T0103974

UNION OF BENEFICENCE
THE WORLD TODAY
AND
THE WORLD TOMORROW

FOR WORLD PROGRESS AND SALVATION

Mohammad Salim Khan

Order this book online at www.trafford.com
or email orders@trafford.com

Most Trafford titles are also available at major online book retailers.

Print information available on the last page.

ISBN: 978-1-4907-6783-3 (sc)
ISBN: 978-1-4907-6786-4 (e)

Trafford rev. 12/29/2015

Trafford
PUBLISHING® www.trafford.com

North America & international
toll-free: 1 888 232 4444 (USA & Canada)
fax: 812 355 4082

CONTENTS

....

Dedicated to my late father Dr. Mohammad Rashid Khan, to my late mother, to my dear wife Shaista and to my children Ayesha, Mustafa, Abdullah, Maymoona and Ahmad.

ACKNOWLEDGEMENTS

All praise be to Allah, the Lord of all the worlds.

I would especially like to acknowledge the hardwork and dedication of my elder two children Ayesha and Mustafa in the writing, compilation and editing of this book. Also I would appreciate my sons Abdullah and Ahmad and my daughter Maymoona for their engagement in the publishing work. I can also not fail to mention the support of my wife Shaista. In fact this could have been not possible without the collective support, help and encouragement of my whole family. May God bless them all!

UNION OF BENEFICENCE

Part 1
THE WORLD TODAY

CHAPTER I
Introduction

The beginning of the 21st century A.D is a good time to take an impartial look at the past, present and future of Mankind. This is a large canvas to cover; and the question may well be asked why such a large canvas to cover?

The answer is obviously the proximity between people and places; this is now becoming a reality because of the surge in Information Technology that is pulling down the barriers that kept cultures and people apart.

Familiarity lessens fears and increases mutual understanding; this is becoming instrumental in removing the horrors of brutality, violence, mass killings and subjugation of one group of human race by another.

Once the specter of war and violence is overcome, perhaps for the first time in its history, Mankind will have a better chance to weigh the merits of the situation. This will only be possible if vested interests are put aside, and it is realized that we are all members of the human race, born from the same original parents: Adam and Eve (Peace be upon them). Everyone will benefit from acknowledging this truth and acting accordingly. This is why I believe that examining the facts is a useful exercise.

Human life is a complex phenomenon with many angles. It is however possible to divide it into a few major categories and to look at the basic factors that will help making our perspective more universal.

Without considering it a philosophical discussion, the following questions are of great significance:-

One	--	What is the reality of this world? And of itself?
Two	--	What is the purpose of our life?
Three	--	Where do we come from and what happens after death?
Four	--	What is true success and achievement?

We will proceed with this discourse keeping these questions in mind. Human life and behavior may be divided into major realms of activity and thought. These are:

One   --   Education, Religion, Values and Culture.

Two   --   Economic Life and Technology.

Three   --   Politics, Government and Management.

Four   --   Search and Research and Pursuit of Knowledge.

It will be helpful to identify and highlight the major geographical divisions of the human race. Without attempting to be controversial, broad classifications may be drawn, such as:-

One   --   The White Race (Western and Northern).

Two   --   The Black Race (Southern and Central).

Three   --   The Yellow Race (Eastern).

Four   --   The Brown Race (Central) which includes

- The Mediterranean (part of North Africa, Lebanon, Jordan, Syria, Palestine etc.),
- The Arab World
- The Turkish World (Central Asia)
- The Indian Subcontinent, Malaysia, Indonesia.
- South America can be classified as Brown or Hispanic.

This is classification of convenience and many areas may be found to overlap in one form or other.

Similarly mankind is characterized and divided linguistically, often overlapping racial and geographical boundaries. English language is increasingly playing a dominant role in human communications. Similarly another important factor for division of the world is based on the legacies of imperial powers like Britain, France, Spain, Portugal, and the Dutch. In areas where the French ruled people speak and communicate in French. The British of course has the biggest colonial back ground.

Here I would like to digress a little, to mention the major problems that have caused mankind great distress and suffering. These are: -

One   --   Wrong beliefs, Creeds, Values, Intolerance, Bigotry and Divisions.

Two   --   Race for Power, Wealth and Conquest.

Three	--	Mismanagement, Bad and Unjust Governance.
Four	--	Misuse of Science, Technology and Destruction of Environment.
Five	--	International Chaos and Discrimination.

It is a psychological fact that we see the world through our own perceptions and complexes. According to my experience the basic idea of this discourse is erroneous as Race and Color of the skin causes more prejudice in the Subcontinent than in the West. I do not deny that there is racism in the West, there is. But the majority recognizes it as 'wrong' and they have laws to protect the victims of racial prejudice; but in the Subcontinent it is not even taken as a crime against humanity to differentiate between people on the basis of Color and Biradari (which is of far greater importance than any human rights).

As for colonialism, it started off as 'trade' to feed the industries and to sell manufactured goods of Europe. The supine people they traded with; allowed a whole nation to be taken over by a handful of foreigners. I guess the truism of 'you get what you deserve' is correct here too.

Race is not the basic factor, nor religion nor caste; Color finally decides in today's world. Take the case of Sephardic Jews; or signs on hotels stating 'Indians and Dogs not allowed' or 'Blacks not allowed'. Religion or caste is not a factor here.

CHAPTER II
The White Man's Civilization

The rise and fall of Europe; a critical historical analysis.The USA/Europe emerging as A Major Power and its thrust towards World Domination.

The past six hundred years of human life have been characterized by the dominance of what I venture to call the 'White Man's Civilization'. Some may prefer to call it the 'Christian Civilization'. But Christianity cannot be defined as the White man's religion only as there are Christians all over the world. It is noteworthy to point out that this civilization is characterized by one and only one special quality that makes it cohesive; and that is COLOR. Race and Religion are not the prime deciding factors although they played an important role in the development of this civilization. History shows that during the emergence of struggle of 'White Man', after the Crusades, Christianity was relegated to a secondary role. The period of Renaissance was again followed by terrible wars between White Men on the basis of nationalities such as Welsh, Irish, Scotts, Roman, and French etc. Or on the basis of race such as World War I and II. Nazi Germany attempted to establish the dominance of what they called the Aryan race. Even in religion the later periods were marked by great differences such as between the Protestants, the Catholics, the Orthodox Church and other denominations of Christianity.

Even in the case of Jews, the Sephardic (Brown) Jews and the White (Ashkenazi) Jews. This really ends the debate if any as no group can be more racist than the Jews (See the book 'Journey to Jerusalem').

Thus it would be correct to say that the de-facto common uniting factor of the White Man Civilization is neither Church nor Race but Color of the skin.

Once again I would like to clarify that it was not always like that and it is only in the present age, only because of communication revolution that man is left with little alternative but to differentiate on the basis of color. We have mentioned earlier that white man used to fight the white man and black man the black and so on and so forth. It is not a law but a transitional basis of the world as we see it today. We are bound to see this change and once the linguistic barrier is broken, we will be left with only one choice, between the good and the evil.

It is surprising that after all this so called 'progress' they have made, while other factors fade into background, Color of the Skin becomes of paramount importance.

This does not speak well of the philosophical depth of the present world's leading Civilization, but what does it matter? It seems to work very well as far as the de-facto political, economic and cultural dominance of White Man is concerned. The only discordant creed of Communism has recently been silenced. Now Super Power status has converged on the basis of color alone.

This is why it is necessary to examine the White Man's Civilization in greater detail.

Europe is the cradle and Greece and Rome were the pioneers and torchbearers of this civilization, forceful and dynamic; they were the most advanced of their time, rich in art, culture, literature, philosophy and science. These societies bordered Asia with Athens, Rome and Constantinople as their major cities. With power and conquest came excessive wealth and luxury and the populace became effete. With the fall of Greece and later Rome, Europe entered the Dark Ages.

Christianity may be called the Trinity based Religion invented by Saint-Paul supported by majority of Jews who wanted to carry favors with Pontius Pilate-the Roman Governor of Palestine and recommended Jesus' crucifixion in place of some robber. Its merger with Roman and Byzantine empires took a strange turn with complex interactions that effected and changed both. While Greek Civilization died, and Christianity breathed new life into the Roman Civilization, Rome branched off to the east into two major centers; Constantinople (named after the Roman emperor Constantine) became the center of Byzantine Empire, while Moscow took second place as the center of Christianity. Moscow in collusion with Genghis Khan was to play a major role as the destroyer of the Islamic World.

During the Dark Ages of the West, Religion dominated the life of the White Man culminating in a tremendous struggle between the Christian and Islamic Worlds. This came to be known as the Crusades (11th and 12th Century A.D).

The Crusades were to have a major effect on the European people. They realized that they could not match or defeat the Muslims who at the time were the largest power in the world (as a result of the meeting of the world's two largest cultures, a meaning-full change began to take place in Europe). The pursuit for knowledge gained importance. The sun set on two people:

One was the religious clergy and the other was the military machine, but it was not for long.

People became disenchanted with religion, and even more with the proponents of religion who however continued to wield power. This power gradually eroded, confining itself more and more to Vatican, seat of the Pope.

The new Protestant sect of Christianity which was founded by Martin Luther gave the final blow, when England's King Henry the VIII declared Protestantism as the official religion of England. Thus the Pope lost power to sanctify the Kings of much of Europe. Nevertheless the process of erosion of this religious power had started. Great changes began taking place in feudal Europe. The dissemination of knowledge with the invention of printing also had a big hand to play in this, as knowledge became more widespread.

When religion fades from society, a vacuum is created. This releases lot of energy which is either suppressed or channelized to other areas of life (for good or bad is immaterial to this discussion). Nationalism now became more important and incessant wars took place between the European countries. The pursuit of power and lust at both personal and national levels became the dominant factors and manmade philosophies became popular in all fields of thought. Norms of politics, economics, international relations, diplomacy, education, social life and morals, warfare all changed. This new found freedom in life and thought created new dimensions. Relationship with God was denoted to a personal affair. Religion and politics separated ways. Rather religion become subject to the temporal powers. The pursuit of power and wealth became the key motivators initiating friction between individuals, classes and nation states. Adventurism, loot, deceit immortality increased though higher values never vanished completely. The foundations of human relationships, social and family structures were badly shaken. The Renaissance, the age of Reasoning, Copernicus, Galileo, Roger Bacon and others renewed the tradition of Socrates, Plato, Aristotle, Democrats, Pythagoras, Archimedes, Ibn-Hazm, Al-Razi, Avicenna and Al-Beruni. The stifling restraints of the Church weakened and science and study of nature were given a fresh impetus. This great field of knowledge about nature and its forces which started in pristine academe purity were to change as the exploitation of nature and its resources also advanced along science and technology. Science and Reason at the pinnacle of the European Civilization was to take a form ugly beyond recognition, as it increasingly became an instrument of ruthless power and destruction.

The great modern tragedy of mankind was going to take shape on the vehicle whose foundations were laid on the thoughts of Machiavelli and has like of political thought which was based on deceit and hate, conquest and power mongering. What happened? What went wrong?

What started as a gust of fresh air - a reawakening of the spirit of discovery and knowledge slowly transformed into another form where this new found knowledge was to become subservient to temporal political systems. Base material gain and the lust for power replaced selflessness and pure ideals. Knowledge, religion, ethics, economics, education and every other aspect of human activity was slowly put at the command of the political forces. What were these new political forces? So long as the feudal system existed the only thing they were doing (most of the time) was fighting amongst themselves. The 30 year war, the 100 year war and many other wars between various monarchies, principalities and nation-states sounded the end of the landed aristocracy and the feudal system. While they were fighting, seeds of the Industrial Revolution, Capitalism and Freemasonry etc. were being sown. Another brand of leadership and management was preparing to take affairs in their hands. But before this Columbus, Marco Polo and Vasco de Gama had found new worlds through their voyages.

Now a strange merger was to take place. The political and military powers of Europe were tired of in-fighting. They started looking towards the vast worlds outside Europe; whole continents were waiting to be conquered. Thus the advent of imperialism and colonialism!

Europe had everything to start the conquest and subjugation of the rest of the world - Asia, Africa, Australia, and the Americas. What riches awaited the rulers and people of various nations of Europe!

The industrial revolution needed raw materials, labor and markets. The capitalists, the workers, the bourgeois, upper and upper- middle classes were impatient to expand and achieve the satisfaction of their desire for power and wealth.

The bursts of intellectual and managerial energy and support of organization based on scientific discoveries giving large capabilities in warfare, communications, banking and mega finance managed, led and put into practical form by cadres of leaders and managers from Eton, Harrow and others academies were the means used to achieve world dominance. Men, money, materials and organizations backed by academic research and formulation of politics methods and techniques unheard of before gave the Europeans superiority in all fields. The creative spirit was not lacking in any field. Even the Church gave its fullest blessings hoping that Christian missionaries would regain what the Church had lost earlier. There was now a good reason to give a sugar coating to the conquest of the world i.e. the noble task of civilizing the 'barbarians' (rest of the world). Business and political ethics and principles were flaunted as never before so that everything legal or not, fair or expedient had to have a principled and legal cover. Behind all this was a philosophy as described by Sir Frances Bacon: "If life is a struggle for existence where the fittest survive, then might is the only virtue and weakness the only vice".

How far all this was from the original principals taught by Jesus (Peace be upon him)!

It is worth mentioning here that this is not intended to be a historical chronicle. Our purpose is to understand the mechanics, the causes and reasons of how European Civilization attained dominance.

Europe was now looking toward far off lands. The process had started in sixteenth and seventeenth centuries. By the eighteenth and nineteenth centuries almost the entire world had been colonized or brought under imperial rule. England, France, Spain, Portugal, Holland, Germany (to a lesser extent), Italy and Russia captured the Americas,

Africa, most of the Asia, near and the Far-East, Australia, New Zealand (and later even the Antarctica and the North Pole).

Local races were either eliminated or confined like the Red Indians, Incas, Aborigines, or subjugated to colonial rule. Political and military rule became well established in the hands of the white men using "divide and rule" and "carrot and stick", 'guns and gold' and even sheer brute force methods. (genocides, nuclear annihilation)

The natural raw materials and human and other resources were captured and placed completely at the disposal of the colonial rule. Huge juggernaut merchant companies like the British East-India Company and Dutch West-Indies Company were vehicles of trade commerce and social systems based on the patterns of the colonizer were imposed in these areas. The pinnacle of this process was the British Empire which was so vast that it was a known saying that "the sun never sets on the British Empire".

Parts of China, deserts of Arabia, Iran, Turkey, Afghanistan and Japan were perhaps the only countries not to come under direct colonial rule though indirect influence extended there too. The peoples and riches of practically the whole world were fuelling the industries of Europe and providing them the means of all splendorous luxuries. The world had never seen anything like this before.

Nature has its own way of balancing excess and bringing equilibrium. During all this process the European people were not united within and great hatred and differences existed between them. In the heart of Europe, in Germany or Allemagne, Austria and Italy another process was raising its heads. These countries including Turkey, Japan, Russia and USA had not found favor with the great bankers who were mostly Jews now controlling the greatest portion of the world's riches.

Adolf Hitter wrote 'Mein Kampf' and attained complete power in Germany through sheer fascist force fueled by clever propaganda. His allies Mussolini of Italy, Sultan of Turkey and Emperor Hirohito of Japan became what were called The Axis Powers. World War I and World War II took place with colossal havoc and destruction which completely broke the back of European colonial powers. As a result most of the colonies were freed but only after being divided into small, vulnerable and dependent nation states. Russia became Communist, so did China, while USA emerged as the major capitalist democratic (free) world super power of the white man's world.

The last fifty years of the 20th century saw the rise of USA as the major power of the world. This same period saw part of the rise and the fall of the 2nd super power Russia. After the fall of Russia, the USA moved quickly to bring China and India into line so that the concept of a Global Village, a unipolar New World Order connected by Internet could be developed. But India, China and Russia as well as other countries have sounded discordant notes over this scheme. While USA is pushing towards a 'global village' under its leadership, not all countries are ready to swallow this pill.

Before we go any further, let us compare the colonial and imperialist powers like Spain, Portugal, Russia, France and Great Britain. In relative terms (leaving aside the harmful or negative aspects of Imperialism and Colonialism) Great Britain showed the greatest amount of tolerance, flexibility and relatively humane approach. They also tried to put up (at least a front) of respect for law, procedure and human rights.

There are no incidents of genocide or brutalities of the likes of mass killings of entire populations. In sex and morals too, they were quite restricted right up-till the Victorian era, and even now I think they are relatively better and much less cruel. Their most dangerous trait however is deceit, trickery and cunning in which none can match them. At the same time it would not be fair if we do not mention their courage, determination and spirit of sacrifice.

Similarly the USA is definitely a better society (relatively speaking) than the rest. They may have subjugated the Red Indians (who were no peace doves either) but you see nothing like the killing of 60 million Kulaks (Stalin era). Time has shown they have more workable, peaceful and efficient systems, at least for the time being.

THE LAST FIFT YEARS:

The last fifty years or more after World War II, is a new era of the 'White Man's civilization'. Major changes have taken place; even now we see breathtaking events and revolutions. The emergence of science and technology gave them new capabilities. The political, social and economic changes matched these in speed and scope. What took centuries to shape was now a matter of decades.

This period saw: -

_____ Rise and fall of Russia and Communism, 'Glasnost', and economic collapse of Russia.

_____ Freedom of colonized countries in Asia and Africa.

_____ Murder of Gandhi; one of the greatest political leaders of this century who introduced the novel concepts of struggle through non-violence/ non-cooperation.

_____ 'The Cold War' after World War II between the Capitalist and Communist Block under USA and USSR respectively, which lasted for almost 40 years and its end towards the end of the 20th century.

_____ Destruction of Afghanistan.

_____ Development of nuclear, chemical and biological arsenals of unimaginable and indiscriminate mass destruction.

_____ Creation of Israel by the help of the winners of the World War II.

_____ Emergence of the European Common Market (euro zone and now the EU).

_____ AIDS; the mystery disease defying scientific explanation.

_____ Rise and fall of the 'Asian Tigers' Japan, Taiwan, etc.

_____ Movement for preservation of ENVIRONMENT.

_____ Concept of 'Global Village'.

_____ Concept of 'New World Order'.

_____ Concept of 'Multinational Corporations' (MNCs).

_____ Concept of NGOs.

_____ Emergence of micro technologies in electronics, computers, fiber optics, communication, robotics, control system, guidance system even into space. The explosive development in genetics. The 'fuel coal' is another land mark discovery. Computing, tracking and surveillance technologies have given an altogether new dimension to warfare. Materials, chemical, biological and precision technologies have brought new vistas into man's life.

_____ Conquest of the Space.

_____ Age of IT - Information technology and internet which is supposed to break the barriers of communications and universalize information, education and economics.

_____ Concept of 'Virtual Universities' (everything under one umbrella).

_____ Concept of the Paper-less society.

_____ Founding of the League of Nations and subsequently United Nations.

_____ Apartheid & its fall (South Africa).

_____ Fall of Communist Poland, the Berlin Wall and the Bamboo Curtains.

The Emergence of Regional Blocks and International Organizations:

A reaction to what is happening in the reign of the White man has shown itself at the advent of the 21st century. This is the formation of regional blocks, based, mostly on geographical vicinity and economic and political interests. Some are supported while others are opposed or ignored. Some of them are:-

_____ European Common Market now turning into a political entity with the abolishment of visa, introduction of Euro - Currency etc.

_____ Eurasia Russia, China, Kazakhstan.

_____ ECO - Central Asian Republics, Iran and Pakistan.

_____ ASEAN - Far East Countries.

_____ AU - Most recently replacing OAU (Organization of African Unity).

_____ SAARC - Countries of the Indian Subcontinent.

_____ OIC - Organization of Islamic Conference.

_____ The G8 - Advanced and/or rich countries.

_____ The group of 77. Developing and poor countries.

And earlier; The British Common Wealth, Comintern (Communist International), The Third World, NATO Baghdad Pact, RCD, ECO and perhaps some others like those based on Arab Nationalism (Bath).

The formation of such blocks on the basis of existing or perceived mutual interest is of considerable significance. Those who have founded these blocks have done so with many expectations. In short, lots of determined efforts have been made to bring cohesion, harmony and exercise greater influence. However smaller divisive influences have stood in the way.

These blocks had many different bases. Sometimes economic and political interests were the common factor. Others were based on race, language, history, religion, ideology culture or plain geographical vicinity.

A look at the performance of such blocks again brings forth the Superpower support as an important factor. Those blocks which were formal with the blessings of the white-man super power be it USA/Europe or USSR proved more effective (in real terms). Others were more of forums to voice common problems. Practically, they have not proved very effective. Still they do indicate a trend which is important from the point of view for future possibilities. It is more like the lining up of large blocks of humanity for a future struggle for greater freedom or influence and benefits.

Here another parallel trend should not be ignored. After World War I the League of Nations was formed by the winning nations to establish an international agency for peace. This however could not prevent World War II. After this War another much more effective effort was made in the form of the United Nations Organization (UNO). Almost all nations are signatory to the UNO charter, and it has become necessary for any country to achieve full nationhood to be recognized by the UN, and become a member of its General Council. The UN has a large canvas which has now extended to two particularly important areas normally:-

(i) UN sanctions.
(ii) UN peace keeping force.

It has of course many other agencies like FAO, WHO, ILO, UNDP, UNHCR, UNICEF, UNESCO etc. which provide policies, guidelines, facilities, and material and managerial support. Some feel that this organization is pilot for the formation of a world government; however its limited budget is a big obstacle in fulfillment of this objective. Major chunk of its budget is provided by USA while its Headquarter is located in New York. The headquarters of most of its agencies are located in Europe. UNO is much criticized for the VETO power of its five permanent members of the Security Council.

Now we come to the third phenomena which is the concept of 'The New World Order' (NWO) given by former president of USA (Ronald Regan), which incorporates the concept of a unipolar world, a 'Global Village' connected by internet and run by MNCs, NGO's, local governments and academics etc. leading to a basic unification in culture, values collective life and interests, under the leadership of USA and its allies with their 'Information Highway', and hegemony in space and sea as well. Now these developments are quite natural with the advancement of technology.

How do these correlate with the UN idea?

A fourth factor is international organizations and movements of another kind such as Red Iron, Green Peace, Socialist organizations, The Church, The Islamic organizations (some peaceful, some militant), IMF, World Bank, Organization for the Unification of Religion, the Salvation Army, The Boy Scouts Movement, Radio Clubs, Red Brigades, various Mafias and many others. All these have an international flavor. While the world is advancing, bitter and murderous nationalistic groups live in another world far behind the times. Look at Rwanda, Serbia etc.

Concluding this chapter about the reign of the White Man, one may say it has taken an international form, while regional blocks and other underground international currents cannot be ignored either.

However the real dangers facing the White Man's Civilization are internal, which are well proven historical facts.

These are:-

1. Love of ease and pleasure.
2. Excessive affluence.
3. Fading away of creativity.
4. Isolation tendency of the masses.

5. Hardening of routines and procedures.
6. Lessening of the real spirit of discovery and adventure. Fear of death.
7. Deteriorating educational standards.
8. Clandestine organizations and lobbies within the body politic.
9. Unstable economic system.
10. The unstoppable Industrial Machine which keeps on mass producing!

CHAPTER III
43 Questions Primarily to the White Man's Civilization

Today whatever good or bad we see, the White Man must take the bulk of the credit or accept the blame, as they were and are the dominant political and socio - economic power.

We the subjugated can only follow or observe this period. All of us have shortcomings still we do have a right to criticize and ask a few humble questions. These questions mostly relate to military, economic, political and social aspects of human life:-

1. Who made the first Atom Bomb and first used it? Who is responsible for the mass production of nuclear and other forms of weapons on large scale, and (which is an injustice in itself) indiscriminate destruction of life and property and the promotion and use of science and technology for destructive purpose (case of Hiroshima and Nagasaki)?

2. (a) The award of the Nobel 'Peace' Prize named after the inventor of dynamite (TNT) Alfred Nobel! What a mockery! This prize is awarded by worldwide producers of dynamites.
(b) Russian government's award to Mr. Kalashnikov by the Russian government for designing the best assault (terrorist) rifle - the Kalashnikov Rifle.

3. It is a well-known fact that the military equipment producers supply weapons to both the warring parties at the same time. Most of these are in the West, USA, France, Britain, Italy, Spain, Brazil, Russia, Czech Republic etc.

4. First countries are destroyed by creating or igniting the flames of war between two countries (Iraq - Iran, India - Pakistan, N. Korea - S. Korea, N. Vietnam - S. Vietnam, Afghanistan, and Kashmir); there is a long list. Then when the countries are thoroughly destroyed, the reconstruction of these countries is taken up and the country is practically put at the mercy and dictates of the powers that be.

5. The killing of 60 million people (Kulaks) in the Stalin era and 50 million in communist China to impose a system which was later discarded by its own

14

proponents. This speaks sadly of this philosophy - a brain child of Karl Marx, a German Jew. China is not a part of the white world but it speaks poorly of their choice of adopting the cruel and Whitman's philosophy of a misguided Jew, nurtured in the cradles of white civilization in Germany and London.

6. An even more unreasonable catastrophe was the killing of 19 million young men on the battle fields of World War I, using Nerve Gas as well. Rise of people like Hitler and philosophies like Fascism are also landmarks of the White Man's Civilization.

7. Which was the last country to officially abolish slavery (USA in 1964)?

8. What were the actual reasons and what was the effect of colonial and imperial rule? Whole continents were subjugated, and in spite of belonging to the same human race their people were degraded to slavery, apartheid, and subjugation. Their national wealth and honor were looted ruthlessly.

9. 'Inquisition' in Spain (burning or killing of Muslims, Jews and women at stakes). An intolerance of completely eliminating whole races. This was repeated in the Gas Chamber killing of Jews during WWII.

10. The contradiction of the support of 'democratic' and 'dictatorial' regimes according to expediency at the same time.

11. The discriminatory role of international organizations like the UN and Human Right Agencies e.g. East Timor vs. Kashmir.

12. The deliberate promotion of classes, racial, linguistic and religious differences and extremism.

13. Effort to destroy local cultures and societies and imposition of their own culture and norms.

14. Little or no protection of minorities.

15. Forced conversion (direct or indirect) from one's religion to other religion or atheism.

16. Discrimination and caste system (e.g. untouchables in Hindus, Black and Brown in Whites) and support of this in institutionalized form.

17. The case of the instability of 'The Greatest Democracy' of the world in the Bush – Al-Gore presidential contest in the Florida State count.

   These are some of the dark spot on the politics - initiatory system of the White Man's reign. The record is not too bright in the socio-economic field too. Some further questions will throw light on these aspects too.

18. Who invented the method of preparing 'heroin', the most terrible narcotic drug?

19. What is the justification for throwing of surplus food (Times Report) in the sea just to safeguard their own farming process while there was famine in other parts of the world like Somalia?

20. Promotion of pornography and free sex on a wide scale even on internet in spite of AIDS.
21. Encouraging sexual misconduct, violence, murder and financial looting in books, films and internet.
22. The dissemination of distorted information and biased half-truths in media, journalism and advertising.
23. Promotion of drug, alcohol and tobacco production and distribution on a mammoth scale. According to some Western magazines China alone is provided with 5 billion cigarettes daily. The hypocrisy of the media and Department of Health's warnings are ridiculous to say the least.
24. Destruction of forests, Ionosphere, pollution of seas, air, rivers, noise pollution, smoke and nuclear pollution.
25. Use of dangerous pesticides and medicines without proper complete trials and dumping them in poor countries.
26. Killing of wild life species for economic reasons like deer, whale, rhinoceros, tigers, and mink and other fur animals.
27. Refusal to help financially the 'have not's' in a proper way.
28. Unfair trade tariffs and unfair trade practices.
29. Selling of outmoded technologies at unbelievable prices and using them for political leverage.
30. Prevention of free inter-country movement for people of poor countries.
31. Shanty towns abound in rich cities. Why?
32. Recessions, depressions, inflation and wide spread unemployment by manipulations, crashes etc.
33. Hoarding of wealth in banks, and prevention of circulation of wealth to promote production and avoid the above mentioned curses.
34. The unliterary manipulation of currencies from New York, Paris and London to bring downfall of whole country economies.
35. Rapidly changing models and producing short life goods. Refusal to provide spare parts.
36. Research in new technologies for dangerous and doubtful purposes like clones, genetic tampering, brainwashing, dangerous bacteria, chemicals and neuron bombs and disturbing rainfall thus bringing drought and floods by disturbing the balance of nature.
37. The unbelievable rate of crime in USA.
38. Highest rate of Suicide in Sweden (followed by Japan).
39. Sympathy for the criminal and injustice to the aggrieved.

40. Prevention of human beings to come into this world through family planning medicines of dangerous types and who knows being secretly used along with vaccines etc.
41. Eating of live monkeys and fish, eating of dogs, snakes and pigs.
42. Superstitions and worshipping of wood, carvings, paintings stones, elephants, monkeys, penis as God or Gods.
43. A remark about terrorism in the world will not be out of place. More than 99% of people who are being killed in these terrorist attacks are Muslims, so how can the Muslims be terrorists?

These are some of the questions which the White Man Civilization will find difficult to answer. They very briefly throw light on their 'achievement'. Can they really claim to have a right to lead the world towards salvation and a 'better society'? Material benefits are the order of the day. Human relations and spiritual qualities are relegated to second and third place.

However we must appreciate the fact that the white man has been able to successfully divert the war like aggressive tendencies of mankind for competition and domination towards the systematic development of the institution of SPORTS.

A look at the White man's personality and their ideal personality

Western white man Aryan civilization is dominated by the "Fastest, Highest, Tallest" Olympic syndrome. The Spartan ascetic going into an unbalanced opposite extreme of power, size and loot and grab (take) and finally to rebel against normal balanced (boring) society, the "lone ranger" type finally culminating into a "brief" community applause to the "hero", the deity like figure who is aloof, different and stunning. Now this goes against all of nature's good and constructive ways and values which if need be rarely goes into the mode mentioned above but is normally a very moderate, well balanced person, humble, giving and avoiding human idol and hero worship trend almost self-effacing (the Prophets were never applauded in this manner).

CHAPTER IV
Chaos and Anarchy or Advancement and Progress

What we have discussed in the previous chapters does not speak well about the White man's civilization. They have fired their last shots and are now merely playing with dreams. The NWO and Global village – unipolar world they propose does not have the entrusted essential requirements for this role. The hardware is notable to cope with the software. The rest of the world is not ready to accept their model given their past track record. This reality should be faced boldly.

We have focused on the White man's civilization be it USA, USSR or Europe which has directly or indirectly ruled the rest of the world for several centuries. What about the Islamic or Muslim world, China, India, Africa and the Far East. As we have mentioned none of these are totally free from the White man's influence in any aspect of human life. This has now become the 'White Man's burden'. He has to lighten this burden by sharing it with his other fellow beings. He has to lead the way and bring matters to a place where a more balanced world picture emerges, where dissensions lessen.

If the White man's civilization can at least stop and swallow this bitter pill, humanity will advance, otherwise every passing decade will see more chaos and anarchy. If the White man is able to perceive this, hopefully a transition can take place which will incorporate the best of all, and shun the bad parts.

What has happened we should forget it, provided the White man is ready to let go the throne and sit down for a meaningful exchange of building a broader based society with all the variety and richness of cultures and traditions, based on truth and merit alone. Let us throw away the mirage and false ideals and come to one basic point alone, that our sole criteria will be truth and merit of the matters. Otherwise we try to fit a square peg into a round hole - it will be a stalemate at best or lead to chaos and anarchy.

The truth and the merit, the wrong versus the right should become the sole criteria of running a new world free from bigotry and injustice. This will be like the fusion of societies through a positive transformation to acceptable partial amalgamation.

I think the time to pull one another legs and use of brute force is over. It should be over. It is time to stop trying to dominate or kill one another. Let us have the courage of forming a 'Democracy of all Nations', the whole of humanity and let merit, truth and fair play be the sole criteria for running affairs.

Why not let go and give humanity a chance to manage its affairs as a whole based on merit and truth alone. Even a child as he grows must be freed. What to say a community of 200 nations, innumerable races, languages and culture. Give the community of nations a chance. Stop the brow beating and remain within the limit.

This is the call for true internationalism based on truth, merit, justice and balance. I am sure mankind has enough sense of right and wrong to go into this. Let us put aside all rational, racial ideological and other differences and come to the point we agree upon; then slowly and surely remove the sore spots; the hot spots which breakup efforts of this kind. Each society must do its own job of cleaning itself. At least bringing themselves to a level where they can talk, instead of kill each other.

How often we have seen this method work at lower levels. Why not at statesmen level? On the basis of truth and merit - case by case. If this is not done we should be ready for the worst or a least linger on in this state - but for how long? The inherent inequalities will not allow for much time in our present situation. This requires a basic change of perception from Us to We. It is difficult but man will only get what he strives for. If we cannot recognize the right and the wrong or do not have the moral courage to stand up for it, then we are not leaders of humanity at any level, in any sense whatsoever.

Let us for a moment stop thinking of ourselves, our families, clans, brotherhoods, our countries, our nations, our ideologies and think of the betterment of mankind with one criteria in mind only. What is right or wrong, true or untrue, just or unjust in any matter, not only mankind, other life forms, in fact even nature and environment (all have suffered badly at our hands because of our excesses) need this approach to survive.

It is the nature of things that one man or one group cannot bring equilibrium and stability. As proved by nature, only God can be unique and alone. Other creations are too weak to stand alone. Nature has created pairs of everything and then woven them into mutual dependent equilibrium. Two points can form a straight line. Three points can form a plane on which a third dimension can create a real figure in space, stable in space and time. On the other hand the present world structure gives a hotchpotch picture with too many inequalities. That is why it gives a disharmonious, ugly look. There is no beauty in the present setup. Man, the lover of beauty and harmony has disfigured the community of nations and disturbed the balance of nature.

How can we change all this? We are not philosophizing for academic sake. We want to work out useful and practical solutions. In my humble opinion most of the problems and wars of today are because of the small countries which are unable to manage themselves properly, and then become tools in the hands of bigger powers which try to pressurize one another by using these small and poor countries.

Much to the detriment of the people of these small and poor countries, the anomalies are great, the differences of standards of life too much. Even basic needs are not fulfilled. Wherever aid is given hundreds of parasites in these societies gobble it up and make matters even worse by daunting donor countries or by increasing the backbreaking burden of debt. Therefore;

STEP I

The first step should be to address the small countries to align themselves as blocks - responsible political entities who can take up responsibilities and who can fulfill commitments. These blocks can be suggested as follows:-

BLOC I	Hespanic block.
BLOC II	African block.
BLOC III	Sunni State.
BLOC IV	Jafferi block.
BLOC V	Great Regional Block.
BLOC VI	White Block.
BLOC VII	Black Block.
BLOC VIII	Islamic Sacred State.
BLOC IX	Greater Turkestan.
BLOC X	Greater China.
BLOC XII	Greater Indonesia.

These blocks are so proposed as to provide the least difficulty in integrating into blocs.

The blocs should able to form a parliament, enact laws, build government, abolish travel restrictions, have common defense and common currency and foreign policy and settle matters amiably between member states. Examples of ECU or EU should be studied closely to evolve practical models.

STEP II

Formation of the World Council of United States which will discuss matters of importance, resolve issues and provide help as needed, regulate trade between various blocks and exchange of currencies etc.

STEP III

All the blocks will be engaged in presenting their respective cultures, methods and create a spirit of healthy competition and good intentions.

STEP IV

Step four will consist of No-War parts between these blocks and general agreement of mutual respect. A code of honor should be signed where each bloc is bound to refrain from harming each other.

Difficulties and Obstacles:

This great transformation will have quite a few difficulties before it can become a reality.

The first difficulty will be to convince the countries within a certain bloc to forego some of their privileges for a greater purpose. The nationalistic spirit will be the greatest obstacle in this process.

How can we overcome this obstacle? The answer is easy. The smallest confederating state will be taken as the basic unit. While the smaller states will sacrifice part of their sovereignty, the bigger countries will be ready to divide themselves in parts which are equal to the smallest population density and wealth which will of course determine the actual equivalence along with other factors weighted in a scientific way so that the division is most equitable.

One state will then be mutually elected for a certain limit on a rotation basis period to have extra weightage in representing the countries of that bloc. All countries will be fully represented in the regional council in every sector and area, so that the representations fully satisfy the maximum need of each and every one.

Secondly the other major obstacles in this process are: (a) Border clash

(b) Problems of minorities.

In this connection all border dispels must be satisfactorily resolved with the full interest and participation of the bigger power as soon as possible in a just and amicable way based on truth and merit. We should go so far as to arrange migration from on part or the other if required. Where this is not possible minorities should proceed under stringent international sanctions. The 'hands off' approach or 'let the devils fight' is not going to have any beneficial results for the bigger powers in the long run. Other security and human rights problems can also be addressed in this manner.

Inter Bloc Relations:

Here a word of caution, the formation of these blocs in no way should mean rigid isolationism between them. Rather mandatory exchange of tourists, officials, media men, business and other should be frequent and easy with wide coverage and plenty of exchange of information. The visit and visa policies, travel arrangements, exchange restrictions and immigration should all provide incentive, and enable widespread exchange of information, contacts and good will. This should also point out anomalies and remove misunderstandings.

A large well-staffed International Bureau of Translation should be available with its representation everywhere to tackle the problem of language as a barrier in communication and understanding. This whole process should be on a gigantic scale, if we are to work for true internationalism of any kind.

Full security should be provided to inter-regional travelers. Same arrangements should be available within the bloc themselves.

The teaching of languages should be given as much importance as the teaching of sciences and other disciplines, only then can we truly transcend the barriers between nations. English is the Lingua Franca but this keeps matters at a rudimentary level and skips the greater part of what's going on.

Problem Spots:

We will now attempt to identify existing or possible trouble spots which will stand in the way of this program of salvation and progress. These are:-

1. Ireland.
2. Former states of Yugoslavia, Bosnia and Albania.
3. Israel and Palestine.

4. Somalia and Ethiopia.
5. North and South Sudan
6. India, Pakistan and Kashmir (It will be very positive if India converts to Islam. This will make it possible to form a bloc).
7. Xinxiang, Central Asia and Pakistan.
8. Afghanistan, Central Asia and Pakistan.
9. Chechnya.
10. Iraq and Iran.
11. Mexico and USA.
12. South American countries and USA.

These problem areas have to be sorted out and resolved before the plan for a peaceful world can be put into practice.

These matters of exchange regulations, tariffs and problems of poor countries need sympathetic consideration to help the have-nots and alleviation of poverty. The economic matters in fact are on top. WTO membership is one example of how serious the issue is. This can lead to revolution in world affairs. Man has been doing everything in the fields of science and technology but the more important matter of human relations and affairs at collective and individual level has been ignored very badly. Outmoded methods, thousands of year behind the time are a disgrace to human society. The principles of sincerity, truth, merit and justice are absent from the field of international relations. Human rights are a joke, people strive and die in misery and pain, while others throw food and devote life to the attainment of personal pleasures. This can have disastrous effects in the not too distant future.

Our approach towards one other should at least be humanistic and helpful to say the least.

Maybe we hope and pray that this happens in the not too distant future. It is possible if a will and determination exists amongst the people and leaders of the world.

An international meeting of all heads of states should be convened after study and improvements in this plan, and the practical steps should be discussed. Life cannot ignore this. The whole future of humanity is at stake. Remember time will come when those who are in power and comfortable will need help when power of nature is beyond their capacity. How will the have-nots react at that time? Will the champions of truth, merit and justice be able to do anything?

Toynbee has well analyzed that if the creative minority is ignored completely into oblivion, that society must die a disgraceful death perhaps at the hands of some unscrupulous brain who may bring together weapons of mass destruction with brain, money and technology to create an oppressive dictatorship or total/partial extermination in a holocaust scenario. (See "Future of mankind" in Unpopular Essays by Bertrand Russell)

We have dealt in much systematic detail as to what the 'World Tomorrow' can be, in a hopefully satisfying manner in Part II of this book.

The White man lived in cold and hunger for centuries in the past wants love and peace. He is caring and loving in a dominating and aggressive manner. This surge of emotion when misdirected goes to sex, power craze and materialistic activities many a times to run faster, higher, taller, and stronger in everything including religion.

The tiny yellow, timid and indulgent brown and savage blacks are no match for them. Desire, love and motivation can be misdirected. This happened in White man's case. Desire, love, motivation, compassion, cruelty made a strange combination. So he went out to bash the world in his love, (we have a saying "A donkey's love is a kick")

By throwing the sword, which is the White man's strongest weapon, he is asking rest of the mankind to join him. The White man did it once five hundred years ago. Let him do it once again with more experience, grace, justice and tolerance, with more giving and less taking.

CHAPTER V
62 Ways to Loot the People

Although mankind has been afflicted with the evil of looting each other due to love of wealth and greed i.e. he has been plundering his fellow man's wealth through unfair means, injustice and aggression. And people are very much aware of these ways such as theft, robbery, stealing, adulteration, lying, financial embezzlement through false accounting and manipulation of inheritance and related matters, hoarding, bribery, fraud etc.

The purpose of my writing is to make the common people aware of those unconventional ways through which they are being looted. A disease can be treated only if it has been rightly diagnosed. Humanity dies a slow and painful death due to the extreme economic burden on its shoulders. Continuous, back breaking, inhumane toil which destroys a man's character and manners, ending happiness in his life, depriving mankind of its most basic and fundamental right and making it an extremely difficult task for him i.e. to earn an honest livelihood, for which Allah has provided all the resources of this universe in great abundance and subjugating the universe for him.

No physical, political or any other kind of slavery is comparable to this economic slavery- curse of mankind- *Fitna-e-Dajjal*. Mankind had been aspiring to become closer to freedom with every passing day, but in reality every new system, slogan entrapped him more and more.

O mankind, in effect true freedom can only be achieved by escaping the shackles of economic slavery. Only then, can you achieve the status of Allah's supreme creation. Allah has created everything in the universe to provide for the needs and service of mankind, for its growth, and development. Instead he has been enslaved to the same means which were meant to serve him.

He has been forced to dwell in filthy slums, polluted air and water, consume contaminated food, and engage in dirty means of entertainment, drug addiction, alcoholism, adultery and nudity. All this has paralyzed his mind and his ability to think. Afflicted by all kinds of diseases, achieving education for the purpose of economic enslavement, entertainment as its trap, and bonded labor which is against his own will and is excruciatingly painful for his mind and body, an unprecedented practice, never seen before in the annals of history even in the times of Pharos- calling the wrath of the Creator of the Universe.

Behold the economic slavery of today, which has destroyed the whole mankind, putting the future of our children at stake, so much so that a poor child is unwelcomed on his birth. Making men fight amongst themselves quenching on each other's blood. The sanctity of man, his self-respect and esteem is being tarnished. Mischief and chaos prevails today. This money game has, sometimes through nationalism, or sectarianism, or religion or often for no reason played with lives of millions.

Custodians of this wealth are not human beings and nature will never forgive them for transgression. But we should remember that, no gains without pains. Hence, first of all we need to understand this game. Doing will then become easy. We need to fight against and finish this satanic devil. We have to struggle and work hard to succeed in this fight and to break its shackles.

Mankind has to let go of for some time, its differences of color, race, time, space, religion and sect, and form a Union of mankind to achieve a single objective - single not in a negative sense. Once again to re-emphasize, the union is not for any conspiracy. This is not an alliance meant for achieving some ulterior motive but for greater good. It will not be forced upon people, it will be beneficial, elevating, and will be based on truth, wisdom and hard work. It will be the union of mankind which cannot be failed through use of force, violence or conspiracy. It will be based on courage, dedication and sacrifice. But in a manner, which will ensure definite success. It is not about taking but giving. This alliance will remove all those lie based systems that form the pillars of the present economic system, be it political, educational, and military, government, administrative, scientific, and technological; and replace them with goodness like a pleasant breeze of fresh air.

It can accommodate all, except for the followers of Satan. Such filth can be thrown away into the depths of oceans, flow of rivers and the breeze of fresh wind; after all this is how the universe works.

Now you will see with much clarity and ease, that how man is being looted:

1. Computer hacking.
2. Theft, embezzlement, fraud and stealing.
3. Robbery.
4. Loot during disasters.
5. Dacoit piracy.
6. Unlawful inheritance.
7. Tax evasion from just governments; this puts the loss on productive people.

8. Unlawful taxation.
9. Adulteration.
10. Unjust measure.
11. Unlawful pricing.
12. Profiteering.
13. Hoarding.
14. Interest and compound interest but still the prices are high.
15. Inflation-Not to allow production and increase in production of essential goods.
16. Depression.
17. Recession.
18. Stealing of government property by the departments themselves.
19. Non maintenance of expensive equipment.
20. Bribery.
21. Passing on the tax burden by increasing end user prices of essential items and utilities.
22. Artificial fuel shortage.
23. To put the country in debt and to go on to a speeding spree.
24. Take the unnecessary loans from banks where we can produce the amount ourselves e.g. they have taken 300 billion dollars in just 5 years (from the total loan of 30 billion Dollar reserves were 12 billion, whereas the annual budget is 250 billion dollars and one can imagine how much money is there in the informal system).
25. Fringing on quality control – 2nd rate copies.
26. Consumerism.
27. Currency manipulation of values.
28. Credit multiplication.
29. Smuggling.
30. Stock Exchange crashes.
31. Mutual Funds fraud.
32. Gambling.
33. Government Bonds.
34. Gold, Diamond, precious stones.
35. Art Pieces.
36. Banking, false loans, false collaterals and write offs.
37. Excessive note printing.
38. Market dumping.
39. Credit write offs.
40. Poor quality short life products.
41. Trade deficits.

42. Wars and destruction.
43. Medical wars and Medicine profiteering.
44. Artificial asset evaluation.
45. Artificial bankruptcy and Bank Fraud.
46. Chartered Accountant malpractice.
47. Reconstruction; first destroy, than reconstruct and loot the country in the process and take over its natural resources.
48. Drug trade.
49. Arms trade.
50. Prostitution.
51. Insurance fraud.
52. "Mafia Don" System.
53. Money extortion by crime syndicates.
54. Real estate Mafia.
55. Timber Mafia.
56. Carters and Monopoles.
57. Fake auctions.
58. Squandering and looting national wealth and minerals, Agro and Hydro wealth.
59. "Privatization" of valuable national assets, technologies and assets
60. Bank 'Freezes'.
61. 32% to 11% interest rate of lending followed by flight or 'theft' of capital to off shore "Wealth Pirates" (like Dubai).
62. Islamic Banking; they will steal 1 trillion from Muslims.

Some Useful Readings:

- Un-popular Essays – The Future of Mankind, Bertrand Russell
- Technologic Trap- Hillary Moss
- Journey to Jerusalem- Karen Armstrong
- Black Holes and Baby Universes- Stephen Hawkins

Part 2

UNION OF BENEFICENCE
FOR WORLD PROGRESS AND SALVATION

FOREWORD

Looking at the state of affairs of the human race, mixed picture emerges. No doubt mankind has made progress in many aspects especially science and technology....

But the picture is gloomy. It would take another book to even have a causal look at the state of affairs and this would lead the reader away from discussing the way out which we are proposing.

And there is a strong likelihood and every possibility that the thrust of the book and the write up will be lost in this study and analysis.

Still this part of the matter is very essential and we are in a loss of how to incorporate this because of its importance on one hand and its depth and expanse on the other. We did not want to put the cart before the horse so the only solution we could come up was dividing the book in two parts. And we have titled this second part as "The World Tomorrow; The Union of Beneficence for World Progress and Salvation. This my dear reader would be the part which you would be reading as you turn over this page. The first part is titled as "The World Today: The White Man's Burden" which dealt with the topics of discourse of Democracy, critique on Nation State theory, critique on United Nations and economic ills and malice of mankind. These topics are so interesting that we will not be surprised that the reader will start reading both parts simultaneously.

Won't you be surprised if I were to say that we are a really outdated race because we are following systems which are thousands of years old and even after much development we exist in a pitiful state of discordant theories and their practice? Mankind has indeed scored real poor marks as far as managing the lives and solving the problems is concerned. Sometimes one leans towards an awesome calculation that perhaps we haven't made any progress rather the way people lived under the Mughal Empire or some other great civilization was much better. I am at a loss to see anything worthwhile in the system of life practiced today and practiced thousands of years ago. Take Rome, take Greece - are we really able to say that we are in a better state?

Systems of life practiced by mankind since thousands of years such as we have the wonderful example of cannibalism, so I would suggest that if the reader is interested he should refer to far worthier life time works of these great historians such as Toynbee,

Will and Emily Durand. It is said that Arnold Toynbee studied 600 civilizations. Just to mention a few what would the reader says if he would be suddenly asked that which system he relates himself to. The Mayas or the Incas, the Indus civilization or the Egyptian civilization, the Roman or the Greek civilization, Socialism or Communism or Capitalism, Democracy or Fascism, Religious fundamentalism or Racism, Terrorism or Cannibalism (sorry I got carried away).

One could perhaps coin some new terms such as killism, warism, bloodshedism. We need to understand that mankind has not come up with a new philosophy for a long time. With all humility I venture to say that I am going to do just that with a hope that the reader will forgive me and swallow his anger for saying so big a thing. Now a bird's eye view of this book as a whole will give additional satisfaction to the reader. I am giving this description to the reader so he can navigate through this part and does not get lost.

This part of the book will commence with the description of beneficence in all its manifestation. This analysis will be comprising of an introduction to the concept of beneficence, requirements for it and a step by step guideline for its implementation in what we have divided into four major areas, which will be comprising of what we call as the Union of Beneficence i.e. ACHADEMIA, GECOMETRA, POLITIKA and ASSOCIA.

A BIRD'S EYE VIEW ABOUT THE CONTENT OF PART II

Two things are needed to be mentioned here:

1. Security and ease of travel
2. To a level of diversity and variety which will be a part of this union, whose shape we foresee as one not being top heaving standing on weak foundations but it will be very strong right down to the grass level.

A whole new society will emerge. At this stage I would like the reader to refer to our critique of nation state theory and United Nations. Essential difference between the UN and the UOB is that UN is an intermingling of Head of States and few others from each country, whereas UOB will bring in together whole regions into what we have called as GRB including their political, economic and social fabric. This may encounter very strong opposition by diehard nationalists, and religious fanatics having vested interests but they cannot and will not be able to stop what is clearly the writing on the wall (I am using the phrase in a positive sense) for salvation.

I would like to forewarn the reader that this is not a work of literature, novel or fiction but we can call it more of a text book or hand book of theory and practice which should be read with concentration, deliberation and comprehension. It does constitute very serious reading. This is not the reading for a few, it is addressed to the vast multitudes of society and should be propagated and promulgated as such in hundred languages which is the need of the hour.

CHAPTER 1
Beneficence

Introduction: Beneficence is the new philosophy and practice which provides a common basis for all mankind to manage their individual and collective affairs in a progressive, harmonious manner in the 21ˢᵗ century and beyond. It will solve many of our problems in a practical manner. The prime objective and thrust of this philosophy is to evolve and practice a way of life in the most beneficial manner of collective and individual benefit for all humans irrespective of nation, language, caste, color or creed; to benefit all creatures in harmony and resonance with nature and the environment.

Requirement: The system of beneficence requires seven types of human qualities.

1) Mercy and Patience
2) Natural Wisdom and Fairness
3) Sincerity and Goodwill
4) Sacrifice and Acceptance
5) Willingness and Hard work
6) Universal Attitude and 'Collective Individualisn
7) Truthfulness and Trust worthiness
8) Cleanliness, Discipline and Order

Keeping in view all of human weakness which is to be compensated by collective and social assistance i.e. collectivism will compensate for individual weakness.

Beginning: All well said, the first natural question that comes to mind is how to start?

The start will be to find the common values and features in the kaleidoscope of human diversity. These will have to be exhaustively, carefully and minutely studied by well-formed and well balanced, wise, broadminded groups of several trained pioneer teams which will thrash out a wide spectrum of matters concerning economy, politics, rights, duties, education, culture, media, science, technology, management, environment, health, nutrition, housing, natural resources, law, international and inter-racial relations, religion; to name a few major categories. Then an <u>initial consensus</u> of <u>common values</u> on the basis of which a proposed 'Charter of Common Values' will be put before the people of the world (the 'global village' of today!) for views and suggestions.

Assessment of Beneficence Repetitive, Adaptive Adaption with constant Feedback Correction:

<u>Who</u> and <u>How</u> will the <u>Beneficence Criteria</u> be assessed - It cannot be rhetoric; or based on insufficient number of sources of information. It has to be a detailed, continuous study using <u>scientific methods</u> involving the common man as well as experts in micro, macro and interdisciplinary science, both in time and space domains; using state of the art statistical weightage, Information; Multilingual technology in collaboration with men of affairs. Greater number of sources will eliminate error to a negligible extent. Naturally the importance of merit, truth and non–prejudicial approach cannot be over emphasized. We may remind the reader that the UOB will be characterized by the participation of the main stream and I would again quote the phrases MULTILINGUAL and MAINSTREAM in bold and capital letters to give them the emphasis they deserve.

We should never forget that knowledge, wisdom, purity of intent, with balance and insight are the crowning glory of man's nature and deeds leading the world to salvation; where long and short term considerations viewed from different angles, areas, fields and groups will <u>minimize </u>damage and <u>maximize</u> benefit.

Let us remove our prejudices and forget our enemies and come to the commonalities. Let us also develop commonalities on the basis of merit, truth and beneficence.

We talk of a New World Order; fight for democracy and against ignorance, disease, hunger and poverty. How can we do that without adopting an open minded approach based on mercy, love and fair play? How can we achieve it when we can't travel safely, speak safely, express openly. Let not the diversity of languages, races, cultures etc. be to kill and damage each other, but to know and benefit each other. Let us honor the life, property and honor of all. I ask - can mankind not pool the resources for supplementing mutual good. Let us go for *Disarmament Armament*. Let us go for using oil to make plastic homes and clothing instead of burning the ozone layer. Let us join hands and minds for common goodness. Let us use technology not for killing each other and fulfillment of desires and greed. Let us remove the bans and restrictions of our thoughts and institutions. Salvation is possible if and only if we can do this.

Jointly the human race has enough men, money, material, management and technology to give everybody a good life - only if we put them together for a win-win solution. Let us not be pessimistic. Let us try or face destruction and anarchy. Let everybody participate with what he has. Change will not come till we change ourselves, clean our hearts change our thinking. Whatever may be said the world cannot go through a reform without;

a) Removing prejudices of all kinds, and adopting merit, truth and beneficence,
b) Education,
c) Communication which includes facilities for translation, clean and safe journeys and stays and ease in visa regulations and perhaps cheaper fares with new technologies.

About education there are many principles which have been discussed in detail elsewhere but knowledge should be acquired in pristine purity of intention as well as presentation. After this let the better things be developed and adopted. Let us for example study all great civilizations. Let us ignore the conquest of others, the pomp and show. Let us concentrate on finding what qualities made the great societies. What values, ways and means adorned their society. What made them decay and fall. Let us learn from History (the accumulated experiences of the people, the society and leaders in all fields).

Let us evaluate what science and technology have done for us. With the resources at our command it should be possible to carry out a new study with all the vigor it deserves for the awareness of a better path to the future.

Dear Reader! The level of variety and diversity and interactivity will be of such stupendous dimensions which mankind has never seen and this will be possible with computer and IT. The number of inputs will be millions and inter and intra human communications will be of a magnitude never witnessed in the annals of the history before. This is why the reader will be surprised to know that the new system of beneficence will be led by Electrical Engineers. They will form the elite service of UOB and will be of unquestionable honor and repute. Just as the Aristotle predicted a Philosopher King, we predict an Engineer King (Democratic King) as in today's world which seems to be frustrating before the idea of Democracy and to use the words King and Queen in today's world is considered blasphemy which seems ridiculous to me because we should not be following slogans which perhaps we even do not understand. Although I have mentioned Engineers but the thrust of UOB is very much on the interdisciplinary multilingual philosophy. The reader will be really interested to know that what this inter-disciplinary multi-lingual philosophy is. The society will function at a level which we might call as the META LEVEL and this will be a quantum level never seen in the annals of history.

This will be a payback time for scientists - those who used their knowledge for the terrible destruction they have wrought on this world and for ruthless and blind unjust bloodshed in their hunger for wealth and for the satisfaction of their base desires for dominance and aggressions. The great age of Renaissance which started as a wave of fresh air for humanity, in 100 or 200 years became the greatest tool of destruction and bloodshed at the hands of short sighted and unscrupulous leaders who used to call themselves as Kings and Chiefs.

Leaving aside all divisions we propose the concept of a Language State which will cut right across the fabric of the whole state population. Inter-language studies will be so common from the primary level that there won't be few translators but nations of translators of at least hundred main languages. This will be achieved through large scale education from the Primary level apart from the education of mathematics (the language of science), English (the Lingua Franca), the regional language, the national language and Arabic or Latin Language whatever the case might be. Society will be transformed such that it will be an extremely interactive society for which of course the pre-requisite is that it will be a multilingual and multi-cultural mass of humanity which will comprise of main streams of whole nations mixing freely through marriages, business and cultural exchanges at mass level. This will require a grand awareness and education program for the promotion of producing millions of multi-lingual people right from the primary level from the flux of interactions. What a blessed world it will be - at least we could breathe in the free world and avoid the horrible spectacle of two extremely intelligent persons talking to each other in elementary sign language. Remember we are holders of interdisciplinary main stream approach which means the engineers and physicists of Interdisciplinary Organizations (IDOs) or equivalent organizations if any (Part of ESLAM²BTLR see explaining below). Of course other groups will be integrated too. MNCs and NGOs will be working under them.

Constitution of IDOS
ESLM²BATLR

E   ⇨   **Engineers (Electrical)**

S   ⇨   **Scientists (Physicist, Agricultural, Social)**

L   ⇨   **Language Teachers, Promoters and Experts**

M   ⇨   **Managers of 3 different types:**

Men of Affairs   (**Public Administration, Bureaucrats**)

Private Organizations Commercial and Non- Commercial Managers

Military, Paramilitary and Security Managers

M   ⇨   Media

B   ⇨   Businessmen

A   ⇨   Agriculturist (Farmers)

T   ⇨   Teachers and Technicians

L   ⇨   Lawyers and Judiciary

R   ⇨   Religious Leaders

The esential qualification for the ESLM²BATLR will be to fulfill the following courses.

1) VUSCIES Course
2) IKEM 25 Course (Integrated knowledge, Economic reliance and Marriage at the age of 25 while looking after parents, old sick and needy people on individual basis)
3) KKK Course (Character, Knowledge and Capability)

This is a decisive and practical thing which I have told you. Here I would ask the reader to digress a little and glance through the appendices "Is there a way out" which is a discourse on Democracy and its deviation. I hope the reader will allow me to say that any human system is open for improvement and we cannot be rigid.

This will be a most exciting, enriching and enlivening experience to learn from each other and to work together for a change. Let us achieve more with less and waste not.

Let the beauty in the world heal the human soul. Beauty in sound, vision, in the description of the unknown, in human feelings and actions; it has been given a back seat. The healing touch of beauty has been relegated. We are deprived of the beauty and goodness and engulfed in the ugly.

Before I proceed with further details, I do understand, many will consider this as commendable, but too idealistic and too tall an order. Whatever, this has to be done! The human race has to move to a higher level or face the alternative... the disastrous consequences which everyone can see to a lesser or a greater extent (This is a basic law of nature). It has to overcome the obstacles and make the necessary efforts, struggles and adjustments to survive and succeed.

Now I would like to put forth for your kind consideration the various divisions and major core organizations which constitute UOB, all connected together in dynamic feedback loops. This I hope to do so with charts and multimedia (multilingual) displays for maximum clarity and simplicity (see chart no 1 Page no: 45) which will unfold into further charts as we discuss each one and its components in detail.

CHAPTER 2
The Union of Beneficence

The **Union of Beneficence (UOB)** comprises of **four major Divisions and nine Core organizations** all connected together in dynamic feedback loops.

The four major divisions are:

1) **ACHADEMIA**

   This division will work in the field of <u>research</u>, <u>advancement of knowledge</u> and <u>human (resource) development</u>.

2) **GECOMETRA**

   This division will work for production increase as well as progress, with the principles of beneficence.

3) **POLITIKA**

   This division will encompass the political affairs, keeping in view the principles of beneficence.

4) **ASSOCIA**

   We are not claiming that we are the only one and we would like to be associated formally and informally with all institutions and organizations which are doing similar work. It has been scientifically analyzed that our system will be unique such that it will have the hardware and man-ware capacity to deal with and to cater for the immense diversity. And herein lies the difference that we have given here – the name ASSOCIA. Our main concentration will be to build a strong foundation on the above grounds.

Each major division consists of further sub divisions and each one of them is interconnected through what we have called as **The CORE**.

The nine core organizations of the "Union of Beneficence" are:

UOB CORE 1 METAPOLITIKA ESLM[2]BATLR[1]

It stands for Council of Reform which is responsible for the overall management and implementation of all parts of the UOB.

UOB CORE 2 WCW-World Council of Wisdom

This will finalize the common values and commonalities after carefully reviewing all research work (Divine sources, Research and Applied Practice, Historical, Political, Social, Economic, Scientific, Technological, metaphysical) and suggestions for the World Council of Representatives.

UOB CORE 3 WCR - World Council of Representatives

This will be the largest representative body. It will be a recognized body and representing all sections, groups, gender, age, professions, income levels, caste, creed, color, languages, areas, geographical divisions, nations and states. It should be the largest and greatest organization of the human race, mankind has ever seen. Its method will be to connect millions and billions of people in a cybernetic understandable manner taking the consultation and participation to its logical conclusion and highest form yet seen. This is the highest form of individual inputs contributing towards healthy collective good. An example of the scale and magnitude can be found in the human body.

The World Council of Representatives is intended to be a quantum leap in the development of the political democratic system in three ways towards realization of the greatest number of the most aware, most responsible and participative individuals. The three aspects are:

1) It will be a Global Democracy transcending the barriers of nationalism, not by demolition of national cultures, languages, creeds, customs or variety rather it will be a positive cooperation based on all the best in its richest diversity.
2) It will represent all possible factions through weighted factors imaginable with a real interaction of rights, devolution of power, responsibilities and resources contributing to the health and betterment of the whole political body. This will go down to a constant interaction between and with all individuals (if processing technology, devices of that capacity with sufficient speed and channels are

---

[1]   See explanation in Chapter 1

provided or as near to that as possible. Technology will help us and serve mankind in a useful manner). The representation will be age, gender, profession, class, area, country, race and language wise.

3. This will lead to a world with greater interaction and communication and travel in a safe manner. It will endeavor to harmonize the individual and the collective life like that of the human body and its cells.

UOB CORE 4 TAEID-UP Talents and Experts Identification, Development and Utilization Pool/Program

This is intended to be the largest classified and up to date pool of human capital / HR ever.

UOB CORE 5 WSCO World Social and Cultural Organization Media and Culture

It is in the essence of global harmony and a gigantic step towards the understanding of creative human behavior and to regenerate it into an understandable art form. It's the way you look at it. Songs and movies; their effect on human life is tremendous and nothing else except for religion can compete with the impact they create. WCO will endeavor to concentrate on the study and selection of the most beautiful and profound films and books produced and written in different languages of the world depicting injustices, the problems and the solutions. WCO will concentrate on the development, production and broadcast of beauty in an undistorted manner to relief mankind from the sickness of the ugly.

UOB CORE 6 WITTSS World Information, Translation, Travel and Security Services (between all major and international organizations)

The primary function of this organization will be to serve as a central hub for exchange of information between all major and important languages through formation of Bureau of Linguistics, World Information and Translation. In each language we will have four categories. a) Literary and Scholastic. b) Commercial and General. c) Scientific. d) Political.

The travel and security section will be responsible for provision of efficient and safe logistics and travel services between different parts of the world.

UOB CORE 7 MITTELCOM

This is the Technical Production and Information Technology (IT) head and heart of the Union of Beneficence which will provide the inter-communication through most advanced information handling facilities. It will have the following characteristics:

1) **Multi-lingual:** This is a much neglected aspect; which, were it not for the English language puts intercommunication at a very low level. This can be overcome by establishing a sufficiently large and efficient facility of linguistics and Global information and translation- WITTS (already mentioned earlier).

2) **Multimedia:** Availability of data and information in various mediums such as print, audio/ video cassettes, images, photographs, CDs, DVDs, memory chips, computers, internet, films, sign displays, outdoor displays, posters, stickers, banners, public address system etc. and using multi-channel, multiplex, and perhaps multi space techniques for their dissemination.

3) **Multi format**: One-worders, one liners, phrases, paras, poems, verses, talks, speeches, lectures, discussions, seminars, stories, novels, dramas, films, scripts, documentaries, discourses, thesis, mimes, audio visual displays, dances etc. This will in fact form a huge maximum level Production House having all sorts of scripts and graphic/ recording / editing facilities.

4) **Multi discipline**: Designed to cover all fields of knowledge.

5) **Multi source:** Information inputs from different sources resulting in accuracy million times even mathematically[2].

6) **Maximum Inter action ability:** Maximum speed for inputs, processing and output (sufficient and accurate).

7) Maximum bandwidths and capacity for utilization of hardware/software.

8) Maximum safety and redundancy.

9) Maximum life and storage (Library).

---

[2] Reference Thanks to Stafford Baer for using parts of his marvelous book "Decision & Control")

UOB CORE 8 - CoReCo Commission of Research and Coordination

This will be responsible for doing Research and ensuring coordination between different types of research organizations; which will be mentioned in their respective places. It will also function as a Reform Commission together with ORIMMSSA DM (for developing weight age and mathematical analysis.)WCR, WCW and TAEID UP experts to advise on the proposed reforms; and strive for their implementation.

UOB CORE 9 - World Economics and Trade organization (WETO): Trade, tariffs, Monetary Markets

Mohammad Salim Khan

Let us look at Chart 1

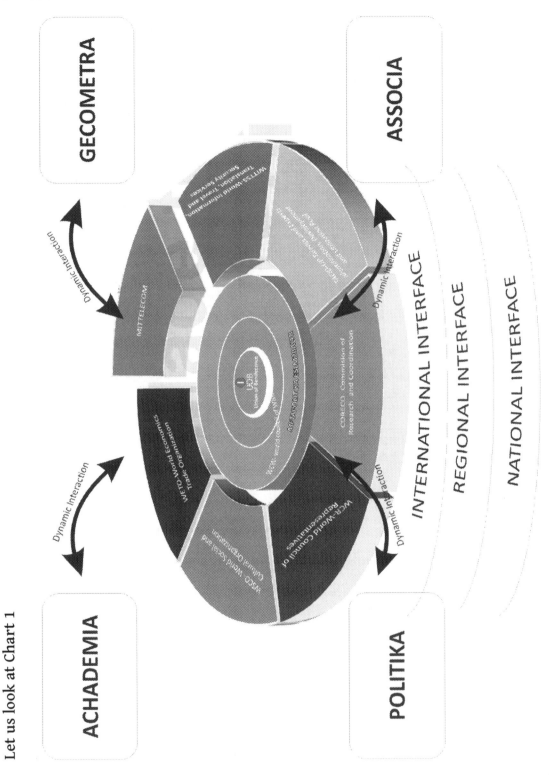

GECOMETRA

ASSOCIA

ACHADEMIA

POLITIKA

INTERNATIONAL INTERFACE

REGIONAL INTERFACE

NATIONAL INTERFACE

Dynamic Interaction

WITS World Information, Transaction, Travel and Security services

MITTELECOM

WETO-World Economics Trade Organisation

WSCO World Social and Cultural Organization

WCR-World Council of Representatives

COREC Commission of Research and Coordination

WCHL World Charter of Laws

UOB Union of Beneficence

In addition to the CORE organizations, the following councils comprising of experts in their respective fields will act as advisory bodies.

- World Executive Council
- World Legislative Council
- Council of Political Research
- Council of Economic and Financial Research
- Council of Managerial Research
- World Media and Communications Council
- Council of Historical and Social Affairs
- Council of Comparative Religion
- Council of Technical Research and Investigation
- Council of Mountain Earth and Marine Sciences
- Council of Legal Affairs and Research

Let us look at Chart 2

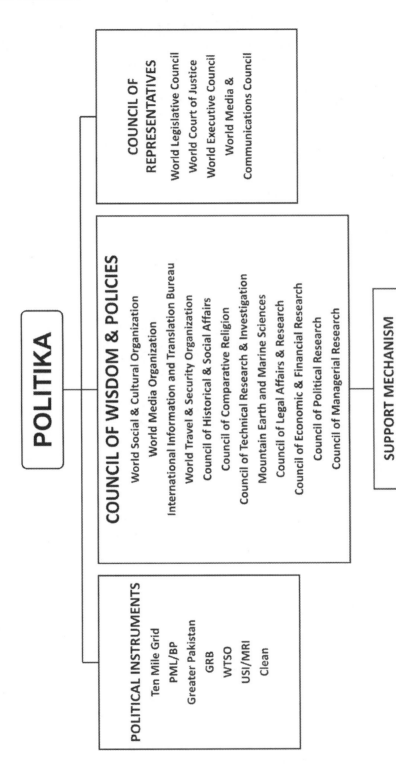

CHAPTER 3
....
UOB Division One

ACHADEMIA - ADVANCEMENT OF KNOWLEDGE, RESEARCH AND HUMAN DEVELOPMENT

There is a definition of sources of knowledge which was made by the great Philosopher poet Allama Sir. Sheikh Mohammad Iqbal. He has rightly determined three sources of knowledge. We may or may not agree but they are; firstly the Divine revelation; secondly History and thirdly Science (Physical Sciences). Whatever aspect of knowledge you may look at, you will find that they fit in one of these categories.

Divine revelation is the knowledge of the unseen. The only relationship between the world of unseen and the universes of the unseen is "life" itself or to put it more aptly 'life and death'. History is the accumulated experience of mankind and science and technology is the rigorous derivation of the laws of natural science through experiment and mathematics.

The reader will surely agree that we are as a whole; humanity in general, has not adopted a balanced and an integrated approach towards the acquisition of knowledge. It is really a tragedy when one looks at the history of human race, the rise and fall of human civilizations, the misery and sorrow which has wrecked horror on the individuals and nations time and again. Now this clearly points to the need of making a supreme effort to overcome this shortcoming. This is one of the necessary conditions of the man's journey towards global salvation in this world and for those who believe in the next hereafter also.

Knowledge is like a light illuminating the horrors of darkness. This matter is discussed in considerable detail with reference to the Greek period, the Arab period and the Renaissance; Glorious chapters in the history of knowledge. In the first part of this book you will also find how knowledge became demonized leading to sorcery, strife, bloodshed, injustice, oppression and suppression of man by man. Here we would like to emphasize more on the revival of the age of knowledge which go hand in hand with the revival of the philosophy of beneficence, and hint at some of the possible methods we need to adapt to what we may call a second revival, seeking knowledge of the world within and the world without.

My Dear Reader! I am pretty sure that you will agree with depth of understanding that the revival of the knowledge is one of the major requirements of the transition from the World today to a better world tomorrow, which is in fact crux of the matter and the gist of what we are talking or writing about.

Here it will be not out of place to strongly emphasize a cardinal principle which in all humility we will try to hint at through some illustrations i.e. the importance of practical application of knowledge for beneficence. Another point with which you will agree is that the sum total of knowledge presently available is lopsided. And much has been lost through the passage of centuries in the annals of history and exigencies of politics and vested interests. So apart from seeking new vistas of knowledge, we would like the researchers of mankind, the men of knowledge to dig deep into the treasures of lost knowledge. Mankind is heir to knowledge; we need to reacquire this heritage. Be at good for goodness sake and be at evil to ward off the evil.

This division will work in the field of <u>research</u>, <u>advancement of knowledge</u> and <u>human (resource) development</u>. It will have three main areas:

1) Research and Advancement of Knowledge
2) Education, Training and Purification 'Tazkiyya'
3) Multilingual, Multimedia Production Propagation (Mu Pro)

Let us look at Chart 3

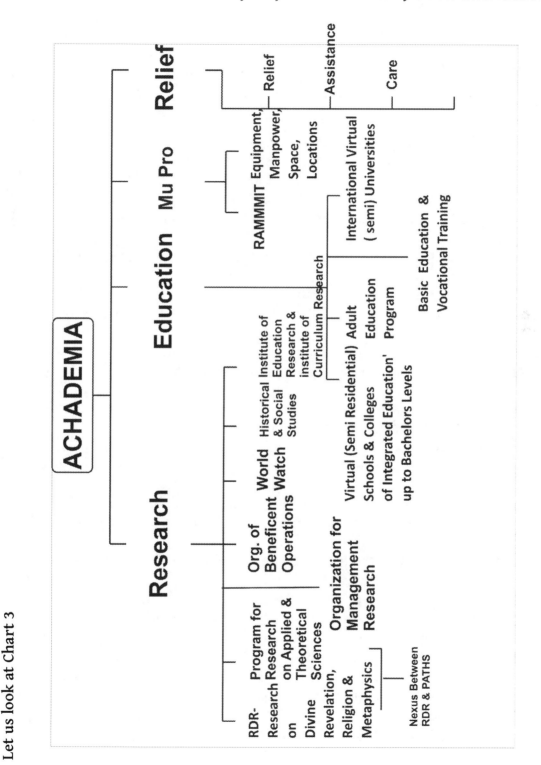

1 Research and Advancement of Knowledge

Research and Advancement of Knowledge will focus on the following areas:

- RDR - Research on Divine Revelation, Religion and Metaphysics
- PATHS - Program of Research on Applied and Theoretical Sciences
- OMR - Organization for Management Research; Goals of Management
- BOR - Organization of Beneficent Operations (interdisciplinary solutions) comprising of information systems, statistical and mathematical analysis, system modeling and system behavior
- WW - World Watch Politics, Law and Economics and Media (Problems, Issues, Trends and Solutions)
- HISS - Historical and Sociological Studies
- IER and ICR - Institute of Education Research and Institute of Curriculum Research

Irrespective of the field of research, following guidelines should be taken into consideration.

1) **Identification** of sources (Books and other material).
2) **Gaining access to** sources identified.
3) Identifying the **format** (e.g. DVD, MP3, print form, online) and **language of the sources.**
4) Where the material needs to be **reviewed**, time will be allowed for that.
5) Arranging for quality translations; also an important task in this regard.
6) Use of computer to improve the quality and speed of research.
7) Preparation of annotated bibliographies, reference lists and suggested readings.
8) Searching for the best team leaders.
9) Selection of talented people for research by encouraging healthy competition.
10) In depth and un-biased search for new fields and topics for research.
11) Resources and technical support.
12) Developing academic linkages with international universities and knowledge centers.
13) Ensuring dissemination and propagation of research and guidance of organizations.
14) Ensuring attainment of consensus on principle religious matters.

1.1 RDR-Research on Divine Revelation, Religion and Metaphysics:

RDR is the Research Program of Holy Quran and Islamic Studies and Comparative religion for the Muslims. Similarly every religious group will do the same and then share. As a Muslim citizen, I would like to give you an example and illustration of the research on the Holy Text. The reader may skip this portion if he or she is not interested in the example. But we would like to suggest for them to develop their own plans of study for their own philosophies and religion/way of life and share them.

An Institute of Metaphysical and Spiritual Sciences (IMSS) will be formed for this purpose. The starting point for this will be the Holy Quran which is the fundamental source of knowledge.

a) Reading, Rules and Etiquettes of Recitation, Calligraphy and review of new styles of Recitation

b) *Tafseer-ul-Quran-bil-Quran-wal-Hadith* **(Commentary of the Holy Quran by the Quran itself and the sayings of the Holy Prophet PBUH) - A Millennium Leap in the Understanding of the Holy Quran:** The basis of this research is constituted by the fact that Word i.e. the Noun forms the basis of knowledge, as mentioned in the Quranic verse;

$$وَعَلَّمَ آدَمَ ٱلْأَسْمَاءَكُلَّهَا$$

And He taught Adam the names, all of them. (Al-Baqarah V: 31)

Key selected words of the Holy Quran along with their derivatives and location charts on the basis of Concordance of the Holy Quran will be collated. In the same manner interpretation of Quran by Hadith (Sayings of the Holy Prophet) and Sunnah on the basis of *Concordance de Hadith* will also be done. All these Verses and Hadith put together in a sequence will present the most authentic meanings resulting in the culmination of Light of Guidance. This will be a rare, precious and extremely useful work and the most authentic interpretation of the Holy Quran.

c) **The Classical Interpretations of the Holy Quran- A Text book for the study of Holy Quran:** The commentary *"Min-Anwaar-at-Tafaseer"* along with the necessary additions from the classical and traditional interpretations (commentaries of the Companions of the Holy Prophet and their followers); also including the background of revealed verses, replicated verses, interrelationship of Quranic verses, interpretation of Quranic words and linguistic interpretation of the verses with reference to the meanings of words in dictionaries, in different dialects and in ancient prose and poetry; on the basis of Quranic reading, recitation, writing, syntax, etymology, eloquence and rhetoric. Word by word and paraphrased translations of the Holy Quran will also be a part of this.

d) *Hashya-e-Tafkeeri-Tafakkur-fil-Quran. Reflections from the Holy Quran:* Interpretations on the basis of knowledge, wisdom and piety. In the next part Allah willing we will be providing the practical jurisprudential legal, political, economic and social interpretations or we may say that the thematic interpretations based on the books of Sunan and their chapters with special emphasis on social, communal, political, legal and economic associations between people. We hope to address the problems of Modern life both in individual and collective capacities with special reference to Quran and Sunnah.

e) **Research Program for the Selection of the Quranic Verses and Hadith:** Research on the basis of different topics and aspects of human life. This is an extremely useful work which needs high level of research. This selection could be categorized as follows:

- Selective *Ayats* and *Ahadith* for prayers, sermons (Friday *Khutbah*) and lessons.
- Selection for women, children, old and youth.
- Quranic prayers and prayers of the Prophet (P.B.U.H).
- Quranic verses and *Ahadith* selected on the basis of topics of books of *Ahadith* e.g. *Imaniyat, Ibadat, Ikhlaqiat, AdabwaMaashrat, Al Qadha, Al Imara, Al Iqtisadiyat, Al Maghazi* etc.
- For media, TV, SMS, Poster, Stickers, One-liner/ Small Para.
- Selection for other professions like Rulers, Army, Judiciary, Media Personnel, Traders, Engineers, Doctors, Scientists, Students, Teachers.

f) **Memorization of Holy Quran - The Highest Level of Islamic Knowledge:** It will start from the above mentioned selection and then will attain the status of *Tahfeez-e-Kamil*. In this, making use of *Tafseerul-Quran-bil-Quran-wal-Hadith* will greatly benefit.

Tahfeez-e-Kamil will be done in original sequence (from Al-Fatiha till An-Naas). Knowing and understanding the meanings of Quran is of key importance for acting upon it (Please see Wisdom of Life - Hikmah; *wa tafaqquh fi din*).

In this way by *Tehfeezul-Quran* the *Hafiz* will be able to know, refer to Quranic verses and Hadith with respect to the issue under consideration and will be able to guide others effectively. Consequently he will become a righteous believer, wise and practicing scholar. He will have a complete grasp over the various topics. As in;

قاری نظر آتا ہے حقیقت میں ہے قرآن

Learning *Qirat* simultaneously is important.

g) **Quran on Multimedia in Multi lingual:**

   i) *Tarajim Sauti*- Recitation and authentic translations of the meanings of the Holy Quran in audio format in 100 major languages.
   ii) *Sair-e-Basari* - **Video Thematic Presentation of the Holy Quran:** The most monumental work ever; Research and Production.

h) *Tafseer-e-Amali* - **Wisdom of Life *Taleem-ul-Hikmah*:** How to act upon Quran individually and collectively; the basis of which will be Islamic Law and Jurisprudence, and chapters of the books of *Sunan* (Hadith Books) with special emphasis on the social, economic and communal interactions between the people, addressing problems associated with the modern times including scientific discoveries, eccentricities, dangers and sexuality both in the individual and collective capacities, and spiritual problems and their solution. The correct application of Quran, Sunnah and Beneficence. For this the following sources will be consulted:

Books of Hadith: Saha-e-Sitta, Moatta Imam Malik, Masnad Imam-e-Azam, Behaqqi, Darmi, Dar-al-Qutani, Mustadrik, Riaz-us-Saleheen, Khutbah-abu-Naeem, Arbaeen-an-Nawawi, other Arbaeens, dhaeef Hhadith, llm-ur-Rijjal, Uloom-e-Hadith. Use of Concordance and similar books.

Books of Fiqh: Fiqh-Madhahib-e-Arba (classical document), Basic books of Fiqh-e-Hanafi, Fiqh-us- Sunnah (Mohammad Asim).

The ultimate aim is to create maximum amount of wisdom and political awareness so that the main stream population can play a correct and vital role in democracy failing which democracy becomes a demagogue and a sham leading to mobocracy, anarchy and purchasing votes and members of the parliament; electable or elected. No nation can make progress in such a democracy.

i) **Research and Deliberations on Other Areas of Islamic Knowledge:**

I. **Hadith and Sunnah of the Holy Prophet (P.B.U.H)**

   i) Review of Zaeef Hadiths in the light of Quran and *Ilm-ur-Rijal* and re-determining their status as sources of guidance.
   ii) omprehensive compilation and correlation of apparently contradictory *Hadiths* and determination of their status.
   iii) Re-evaluation of fabricated *Hadith* and their compilation after thorough research.
   iv) Writing easy to understand but well researched books on *Uloomul-Hadith.* (science of Hadith)
   v) Writing of quality books in negation of rejecters of Hadith.
   vi) The legal standing of Sunnah and Hadith.
   vii) The reality of jurisprudential differences and their limits.
   viii) Definition of Muslim and Ijamah(consensus) on it. What is Fasad? The reality of *Amar-bil-Maroof-wa-Nahi-An-il-Munkar,* Jihad and Qital.

II. *Islamic Jurisprudence*

Recompilation of Jurisprudence, and extractions of detailed lessons from the teachings of Holy Quran, Hadith, *Sunnah* and *Seerah* through thorough research; and preparation of guidance for practical and theoretical realms in a comprehensive manner on its basis e.g. inheritance laws, marriage and divorce laws, prohibition of interest, issues pertaining to blood money, punishment for corruption etc. This would be done through careful and accurate review of the societal problems with special attention to the limits set by Allah and the way of implementing punishments

III. *Seerat-an- Nabi*

Studying Prophet (P.B.U.H)'s personality in general sense, and in different roles (e.g. Husband, Father, Leader, Commander-in-Chief, Legislator, Judge, and Administrator) with reference to *Ibadaat*, manners, piety and generosity etc.

IV. *Sair-e-Sahaba*

Study on life of the Companions (R.A) of the Holy Prophet (P.B.U.H)

V. **Re-evaluation and Recompilation of Islamic History and World History**
VI. **Study of Logic**
VII. **Comparative Religion**

e.g. Works of *Usmani, ZakirNayek*, Deedat, Karen Armstrong.

VIII. **Teaching of Arabic**

Let us look at Chart 4

Let us look at Chart 5

1.2 PATHS Program of Research on Applied and Theoretical Sciences:

This will be the mother organization for research on physical, natural (bio) and social sciences in the Institute of Multi-lingual/discipline Engineering Technology and Science Studies (IMMETSS).

i)   Theoretical Sciences

Mathematics, Astronomy, Gravity, Time, Relativity, Black and Brown Holes, Beginning and End of Time, Life Sciences, Biological Sciences, Relationship between essence of Life and Communication, Genetics, Dualism, Singularities in Mathematical Equations, Metaphysics, Probability and Uncertainty.

ii) Applied Sciences

1) Air Pollution Control
2) Drinking and Agro Water resources
3) Land conservation and development
4) Mega polis revival
5) Food and Nutrition
6) Prepare Foods
7) Ecological Balance
8) Forest and Orchards (Royal Empress)
9) Horticulture
10) Edible Oils
11) Marine source
12) Animal and Botanical Disease
13) Integration and Supplementation
14) Housing, Heating and Cooling- Earthquake safety
15) Hygiene
16) Insect, Fire protection
17) Fuel Cooking, Heating and Cooling
18) Clothing for cold and hot area
19) Bacteria and Virus repellent clothes
20) Process Energy and Materials
21) Mountain Science
22) Earth Science
23) Rivers and Seas
24) Uses of Nuclear energy - Export Electricity

25) Mining
26) Space
27) Telecom
28) Information Technology
29) Robotics
30) Molecular Research
31) Pharmacology
32) Genetics
33) Health care
34) Military Disarmament, Armament, Surveillance and anti-Surveillance - Non Lethal Weapons
35) Ethical Issues

NEXUS BETWEEN RDR and PATHS:

- Contradiction and Co-relation between Science and Divine Knowledge which will include reconciliation of Religion through study of religion, science and history.
- Is religion true? Scientific correlation and religious experiences.

1.3 OMR Organization for Management Research:

Goals of Management.

1.4 BOR: Organization of Beneficent Operations:

Interdisciplinary solutions comprising of information systems, statistical and mathematical analysis, system modeling and system behavior.

1.5 WW- World Watch:

Politics, Law and Economics and Media (Problems, Issues, Trends and Solutions)

i) IPSR-Institute of Political Studies and Research
ii) ILSR-Institute of Legal Studies
iii) IER-Institute of Economic Studies and Research
iv) WCO and MR - World Cultural Organization (Literature, Films and Sports) and Media Research

1.6 HISS- Historical and Sociological Studies:

i)   Critical review of World History
ii) Missing Links
iii) Hidden History – Distorted facts

1.7 IER and ICR- Institute of Education Research and Institute of Curriculum Research:

i)   Basic Education
ii) Vocational Skills
iii) Character Development
iv) Teachers Training
v)   Curriculum Research
    a) Goals of education
    b) International and local curriculum
    c) Proper approach to languages
    d) Factors impeding proper education- contradictions in the curriculum
    e) How to make education time shorter

2 Education, Training and Purification 'Tazkiyya'

2.1 BEVOC- Basic Education and Vocational Training:

Training Schools for children especially for the poor children in fields like:

1. Auto and Construction Machine mechanic, diesel engine, pumps, Agriculture Machine
2. Welding shop
3. Plumbing shop
4. Carpenter Shop and Wood polish
5. Handicrafts
6. Auto Electrician
7. Electrician/ Wireman/Motors/Pumps
8. Mason
9. Sewing and Cutting and Knitting
10. Cooking and Catering, Nutrition
    a. Children

    b. Old

    c. Diabetics

    d. Blood pressure

    e. Hepatitis

    f. Youth and adolescent

11. Tape, TV, Cassettes, Dish, CD etc. fitting and Servicing
12. Driving (light and heavy)
13. Library Science
14. Quran Cassette and CD Recording/ Copying
15. Video Filming/Copying
16. Computer Secretaries - composing in English, Urdu and Arabic
17. Nursing, Physiotherapy, Midwife, First Aid, Homeopathy and Bio-chemic Treatment
18. Health and Nutrition Program Course Conductors
19. Civil Defense, Holocaust Management, Boating, Swimming, Fireman, Navigation, Life guard
20. Guard, Gunman, Weapon Safety, Maintenance and Repair
21. Painter
22. Shopkeeper and Accounts keeper (basic book keeping)
23. Nazra, Qirat, Tajweed, Translation, Hifz, Namaz, Azan, Basic Islamic Course
24. Ethics and Human Relations
25. House wife Household Chores
26. Janitors- Scientific Cleansing

2.2 AEP- Adult Education Program

2.3 VUSCIE- 'Virtual (Semi Residential) Schools and Colleges of Integrated Education' up to Bachelors Levels

The aim of VUSCIE is to bring together excellent teachers and facilities for grooming children into well balanced, attractive personalities with character, confidence, self -reliance, knowledge and skills. A practical approach towards life will be developed in the child so that he is able to face and sustain the challenge of life and be an asset for his family and nation. Social emphasis will be given to the development of better human relations and positive traits in social, personal and practical life.

The education philosophy and methods of VUSCIE are as follows:

1. Unity, Faith and Discipline.
2. KKK (Character, Knowledge and Capability).

3. IKEM 25 (Islamic education, Knowledge and skill, Economic earning ability, Marriage at 25 years).What is the sense of educating your children for 20-25 years and then no application for them, family or country. So the marriage of money, technology and talent is inevitable. There is no other way except to perish slowly and surely. This accelerated program if adopted can give Pakistan 300 million man years in one generation alone. What a tremendous change this can bring.
4. Non-sectarian, broad minded and modern education in a caring but disciplined atmosphere.
5. Cultivation of collective manners and spirit of service and sacrifice with focus on individual abilities as well as human relations.
6. Montessori up to class 5th with certain indigenous modifications to enkindle the faculties of mind body and soul, to develop creativity initiative and depth of understanding.
7. The overall aim will also be to develop in the child an understanding of concepts and mastery over the subjects and skills and learning of languages especially English and mathematics (language of science). Emphasis on study of history, biographies, general knowledge, literature and sciences.
8. Ethical education and special training in human and social relations to equip the child for his future personal family social and professional life with practical guidance.
9. DEEMAPs: Definition, Explanation, Examples, Methodology, Application, Presentation and Symbols system in teaching of science subjects.
10. Technical education, special education for selected children with scholarships and career planning.
11. Tutor system where each child will be given personal attention and problem solving tips sessions.
12. Counseling sessions and career guidance.
13. Short courses, seminars and lectures by prominent personalities.
14. Exhibitions and tours.
15. Healthy competition in games, debates and other co-curricular activities.
16. A proper blend of technical, social education and physical fitness program.
17. Islamic education, *Hifz*, *Tajweed*, Arabic language, Hadith and complete Islamic education package (covering all important requirements).

Other features and facilities:

1. Multimedia curriculum and educational research center.
2. Teacher training center.
3. Good and friendly management and administration.

4. Highly qualified and highly paid teaching staff with spirit and personality.
5. Best accommodation.
6. Heating and high standard living facilities of modern design.
7. Five times prayer in mosques (early rising and early sleeping habits).
8. Vast libraries, some of the best collection of books, print and electronic multimedia.
9. Language labs.
10. Latest computer labs, internet and program libraries.
11. Extra-curricular activities and special education including non- formal education, specially meeting or reading about great personalities, short courses and programs, seminars and exhibitions.
12. Workshops, educational tours, clubs and societies such as photographic, botanical, geography, history etc.
13. Social Work (tree plantation, environmental awareness).
14. Games, riding, archery, hiking, physical fitness, sports complex.
15. Medical care, modern and well equipped basic hospital with qualified doctor, staff, ambulance, first aid, emergency unit and indoor beds etc.
16. Food policy (nutrition and hygiene for best growth, health and piety)
17. Regular holidays, visits, picnic trips and parent meetings.
18. Guest house for parents
19. Dress Code

VUSCIE will incorporate the following special schools too.

i) LTS- Leadership Training Schools
ii) RTS-Research Training Schools

2.4 IVU- International Virtual (Semi) Universities

3 Relief, Care and Assistance

3.1 Relief

WF-DMRR World Fund for Disaster Management, Relief and Rehabilitation

Specific projects and their brief description in WF-DMRR are:

3.1. a. World Development Fund:

For Funding and Efficient Financial Aid and Efficient Utilization

3.1. b. Disaster Management:

In Wars, Genocides

3.1. c. Relief Organization:

For Relief Management and Methods, International Cooperation, Relief and Media

3.1. d. Rehabilitation

Reconstruction, Technical Aid, Legal Aid, Human Rights, Marketing Umbrella

3.2 Care:

Government and the Society will be responsible for taking care (food, shelter, treatment and therapy) of the old, weak, needy, orphans, poor, sick, crippled and those in distress. For this dedicated staff at every union council will monitor their area and maintain authentic and updated records. Elder citizens will be given blue passports and young will support the old especially, daughters and sons.

3.3 Assistance:

3.3. a. Youth Incentive and Utilization Program-YIP (18-50 years)

Every educated person will be provided employment by the government, worth at least Rs.10, 000/ per month.

3.3. b. Parents Compensation Program PCP (above 50 years)

The government will pay Rs.1 million in compensation to every parent whose child has completed 16 years of compulsory education except in case of family business in which the child works. The child will pay Rs.0.5 million extra to his/ her parents on completion of each higher education degree or work in lieu of the amount payable.

4) Multilingual, Multimedia Production Propagation (Mu Pro)

The Muslims populace/masses are in general illiterate and unaware of the fundamental teachings of Islam, – the Quran and the Sunnah. The message of Truth needs to be communicated to educate the people using all possible means of modern technology.

The Muslim Ummah is torn apart by divisions of different kinds. The sectarian, linguistics, nationalistic and regional differences have created an atmosphere of discord and strife where all energy and effort is wasted. There is a crying need to break all barriers, to communicate and understand each other, and to live and work with each other on a practical plane.

The decline of morality is a major cause of concern. No society can progress without a workable social philosophy based on the fear of Allah and the concept of the Hereafter. Self-sacrifice for collective and greater and noble causes is the need of the hour.

Society in general is suffering from great socio-economic problems. The world is now waiting for the transition from the theory and ideology of Islam to its application in the form of practicing individuals and collective institutions in all and every aspect of human life, failing which no salvation of mankind can be foreseen.

The after effects of the colonial domination of the previous centuries have left the present day Muslim societies in a state of mental and physical inactivity. On one had the urge for spiritual awakening and advancement is absent, while on the other the desire to master the forces of nature, and work for real material progress is lacking in its correct perspective with the will to discover, explore and conquer the worlds within and without.

The full benefits of technology are yet to be reaped. The potential of technology and professionals lies un-utilized and without a channel or direction in the absence of a mandate for them to use their talents for the cause of Islam.

The review of the present situation indicates that some CATALYTIC efforts are needed to supplement and accelerate the work of the Islamic struggle. Al-Fajr is established with a view to provide this catalytic effort and to initiate and establish a chain reaction of reform in society.

4.1 RAMMMIT- Al Fajr Research, Multimedia, Multilingual, Multidisciplinary Information Technology

It is an organization established for communicating the message of Islam to different strata of society in an effective and widespread manner, in the context of the realities of today. It has been established for using TALENTS and TECHNOLOGY for the cause of education and research, and the acquisition and propagation of knowledge. It is committed to carry on activities free form sectarian and other prejudices and group differences and to try to harmonize different spheres to the greatest extent within the framework of truth as defined in the Quran and Sunnah. It is NOT a new party created in addition to so many already existing, rather its aim is to serve the Islamic cause, the cause of Allah and humanity, by undertaking necessary efforts (not identical rather supplemental) to support and cooperate with groups and individuals working for the same cause. It is an inter–region and multinational organization in its extent and scope of activities. It is a NON-PROFIT organization registered as a Trust under the laws of the Government of Pakistan.

Al-Fajr envisages the following program to achieve the objectives outlined above:

- To establish facilities and organization based on modern knowledge for the acquisition, storage, processing and exchange of knowledge and information, with all necessary 'Informatics' hardware such as audio-visual equipment, a publishing and printing facilities, computers etc., and other scientific means and methods useful for the purpose. The **"Quran Audio Cassette and CD/DVD Project"** has been the first step in this direction.
- To sponsor and carry out research and study on issues and matters of importance to Islam and the nation and to establish libraries and academic centers.
- To establish model educational institutions and to develop model human resources well equipped in all moral, educational and professional requirements to serve the cause of Islam in an appropriate manner.
- To work for the development and management of human resources and institutions in general.
- To serve as a forum for the service of Islam through exchange of different views, to welcome creative ideas and to plan and implement them.
- To carry out all such measures, financial, organizational and others, that are necessary for the achievement of the above objectives.
- Large number of Holy Quran Audio translations will be prepared and distributed in schools, libraries, as marriage dowries, given to pilgrims returning from Hajj as in Hajj educational package, in local councils, to mosques, hospitals and individuals and organizations (like transport unions and agencies), government departments all over Pakistan in a proper and well organized manner.

The key characteristics of AMMIT will be:

- Multipurpose/ Multichannel
- High speed
- Multimedia

- Multilingual (3000 languages)
- Formulation capability(Message)
- Continual Research
- Interactive high capacity dialogue
- Interdisciplinary multiple department (Multiplexing, Queuing, Routing)
- Highest Diversity
- Internet
- Broadcast
- Radio and Satellite, Mobile telephone
- Real Time domain;
- All purpose

All possible media of communication would be utilized including but not limited to:

- Print (Hard Copy)
- Electronic media products
- CDs /IPods

4.2 Equipment, Manpower, Space, Locations

Various stages involved in the propagation are:

- Reception and Acquisition
- Translation
- Recording
- Classification and Editing
- Storage
- Retrieval
- Packing
- Parceling
- Mass Scale distribution
- Space Domain
- Media Forming
- Media Formatting

- PROBRONET Complex
  PRO – Production (highest variety, quality and formulation and diversity)
  BRO - Broadcast (radio FM, STV, CTV, Mobile Telephone)
  NET – Internet (broadest, quickest, highest capacity and speed)

- ○ DUDIEPAW COMPLEX
  DU – Duplication (mass level)
  DIE –Distribution

- ○ Base Camps (Workshops, Factories, farms, Stores, Vehicles)

CHAPTER 4
UOB Division Two

GECOMETRA

Introduction

Life revolves around the economic needs, wants and requirements of human beings. The extent of these requirements for human beings is far beyond any other species. It is an insatiate appetite for more and more leading to a state of imbalance which goes so far to the extent of endangering the environment and echo systems.

I am tempted very much at this stage to put before the reader a detailed account of the malpractices and wrong doings of mankind in this area particularly. But the tone of this book is positive and one of hope, and I don't wish to change this pattern. Therefore I have addressed these matters in much detail in part 1 of this book "World today" which the reader may refer to from time to time.

I would not like to use harsh words but I am sorry to say that throughout the history except for some occasional bright spots man has behaved like a ferocious animal stopping at nothing to get what he desires using all means fair and foul. It would not be inappropriate to say call him an Economic Animal rather than an Economic Man. However let us turn our attention to more important matters of how to solve and improve the situation. A tall order I tend to agree. After years of deliberation I have come to the conclusion which is not new and has been already propounded by men more learned than me: that the wealth of the nation depends on three factors:

1. **The Material:** for wealth of a nation is derived from earth itself whether we till it or dig it. It all starts there. The 105 elements lay down in the periodic table are all found there.

2. **The Man Power:** who is been given the viceregency over the matters and materials of nature (even energy is a form of matter).

3. **The Increase In Wealth/Production:** created by human efforts put in the material. One farmer, one craftsman, who gives a finished product, creating surplus value.

All of this has been discussed in detail in Marx's epoch making book "Das Capital" which for centuries changed the course of man's economic ventures. It was a brilliant analysis he called this surplus value; The Formation of capital. In communism the capital belongs to one state, which in capitalism belongs to the elite. But he made two big mistakes:

1. He ridiculed religion by labeling it "Opium of the Masses" and denied the existence of God —How far a man can go?

2. All his writings were influenced by one Industrial Revolution which he witnessed around himself in Europe which was a small mass which subjugated and captured most of the world's wealth and he conveniently forgot the agrarian societies i.e. much of the human population indulged in agriculture.

That is why Mao proved to be a greater leader than Karl Marx's prodigy Lenin and Stalin.

Whatever the case may be the fact remains that with the greater integration of society there is an increase in population and a demand for sophistication in goods. There is a need to enhance the production of under developed and developing countries. This is our greatest economic failure with the exception of China, while at the other hand the developing countries are over producing and wasting and forcing their goods on the societies who don't have the buying power to purchase them.

Thus we see this ironic situation where a man is not able to build a two room house for his family and on the other hand every member of that family will own a car, rammed down their throats just because they are produced and marketed by a developed country and on top of that fueled by the Black gold, the fossil fuel whose prices have increased from 4$ to 100$ in last few decades.

How rich will these countries get and how poor will they make these developing countries. Is there any end to this greed? Isn't it insanity that one person should have everything more than he requires and the other shouldn't have anything, not even his basic needs.

Where is the Philosopher King of Plato, where is the Philosopher King of the Elders of Zion? Where are the ideals of the American constitution? Where is the "love thy neighbor" of Jesus. Where is the New World Order propounded by Bertrand Russell on one coronation of Queen Elizabeth-II? Where is the much founded role of MNCs who are willing to spend six billion dollars like Vodafone to promote the casino of cricket but who are not willing to put a 100,000 dollars for reconstruction of schools for poor people.

Ladies and Gentlemen, let us never ever forget that actions depend on intentions. Sincerity and well wishes is the name of the game. That is why whether you like it or not, accept it or not, Beneficence is the philosophy for salvation of mankind. All other issues and philosophies are old and tested. This one is new. It has a source but we will not discuss it.

Coming to the topic, the white man likes to be the ruler and the china man would like to be the producer. What about the rest of humanity. Asia, Africa, South America? What is and will be their role? Are they going to be the markets where developed countries will develop their goods? But where is the buying power? These areas are poor in everything except Human Resource which is in abundance, perhaps $3/5^{th}$ of the entire human population which is lying near the poverty line. It will not be an exaggeration to say that the economic picture is very gloomy and bleak.

Now I would like to refer you to the New World Order particularly its economic aspect. It was thought that the Multi-national Organizations would be the torch bearers of the economic activities of the New World Order, and we have been observing this proclaimed leadership for many decades. The problem as we have just mentioned is this $3/5^{th}$ of humanity living around the poverty line with no buying power. So what do the MNCs do as the instruments of the rulers i.e. West and China/Japan including Russia as they have always enjoyed a romantic relationship? Sir, I digress and beg your pardon.

In the following pages, I have tried my level best to lay out in comprehensive detail a wide array of economic activities but in what framework? Looking at the growth of MNCs which takes its manpower and raw material from cheapest sources at such a gigantic scale that it is not under any competitive pressure, it was reasonable to assume that from their billions of dollars budget, they would run the world in collaboration with the local government and communities. Even the term Corporate Social Responsibility was coined but no CSR initiative of any significant impact was witnessed. The pathos; the business man way of thinking of just making profits.

For example while observing various TV shows in which the telecom joint Vodafone committed an astounding figure of 600,000 billion Indian Rupees to the development of 12 giant cricket teams and centers. It really astounds me in a country where people don't have clothing, housing, water food yet MNCs are sponsoring the cricket league with such astronomical amounts. I kept asking myself that out of all the things in the world, a huge commercial giant investing such an amount in a meaningless venture which is almost criminal. The only reason that I can find is that the MNC committed this amount for setting up a global cricket casino where they will manipulate even bigger sums. Otherwise in the wake of the horrifying problems that India is facing, this seems absolutely absurd. If this is the way the MNCs are going to run the New World Order, then we can say goodbye to the system even before it prevails.

Before I go into the money earning and skill development among the masses, increase in production and control of prices, there are two things I would like to mention. One is while the developed countries have brought down interest rates to almost zero percent (1-3 % amounts to service charges). Even a term ZIRP (Zero Interest Rate Policy) is coined for it while the underdeveloped countries are struggling with rates as high as twenty percent. If this is the way that the underdeveloped will be kept as slaves and some countries will grow richer and others will grow poorer and indebted by international monetary agencies. With these interest rates the population can never contribute to increase in wealth of nations. A stagnant capital flow slows down the economic growth. The Keynesian method of zero percent interest rose USA from the great depression augmented by an adult literacy program started by President Ford. Through Ann-Arbor studios thirty million Americans undertook the adult education course comprising of two parts.

1) Skill development

2) Awareness courses which gave people an understanding of their constitution, government, history and self-esteem.

Same has happened in China recently. The Chinese only knew how to make locks and bicycles but as the West gave them technology (now they are living up against USA).

As long as the Nation state exists, and GRBs are not formed to be discussed in subsequent chapters, GECOMETRA alone cannot solve the economic problems. I have emphasized the need of skill development for any nation to contribute to the well-being of humanity for example if China is the new production leader, then Pakistan can be the food basket so that they should supplement each other, not compete but complement each other's shortcomings. Let's again take a very hot topic that is the transit route from Pakistan. Pakistan should be given the transit fees like the Swiss Canal or Panama Canal. This could be called the Chinese transit. Trade agreement and the overall management should be given to U.S so that everybody gets a piece of the cake (win- win). The only reason this won't be done will be something ugly underneath the surface. Let US and Europe take note of tremendous snows in their continent. Even if you don't believe in God, you will believe in retribution of nature. What goes around comes around.

Having said, coming to the second point which deals with Meta-Physics. I am now going to state something surprising but it based on the findings of the greatest scientific minds - Einstein and Hawking. This is based on "the faster a thing moves, the bigger it gets and vice versa." At the speed of light mass becomes infinite and space loses its meanings. But if you are at the other end of singularity (+/- infinity), don't forget you can end up at the other end of a black hole crossing galaxies in zero time. That is why we believe in some great principles like "Give – Don't take", "Use it or Lose it", "Start with what you have", "Make the best use of thing", "Earn by producing not plundering", "Towards beauty and cleanliness", "Achieve more with less", "We win you win", "Knowledge - Wisdom - Balance - Perseverance - Action." These are few phrases which included the philosophy of Beneficence. Now I will deliberate upon the most striking statement, "**Your Wealth increases by giving not taking**." Wealth is like a mass, the more you give the more space you create and the quicker you give the quicker the space grows.

One may not realize that you want to do something for one billion dollars, instead you gave it to someone who had one trillion dollars and he did it by spending 100 billion dollars. This is how just an idea is exponentially enhanced, an act of goodness is exponentially enhanced many folds. That is why all great men, nations, Prophets, God Himself keep telling you to spend the wealth in a balanced way and discourages amassing wealth. This requires some philosophical deliberations and I will request the reader to stay with me.

In the animal kingdom, those species that eat others gradually become extinct, e.g. lions, leopards and sharks while those who feed others are increasingly abundant like goats and cattle. Similarly those species that only feed themselves and are of no use to others also became extinct e.g. dinosaurs. Coming back to the topic I would like to elaborate a little more on one principal of supplementing and complementing. Let us assume that Australia can produce enough wool to cater for the whole world. So I shall not start sheep farming, being unnecessary duplication. May be there is shortage of meat, so my country should instead go for animal husbandry. It is this consultative process, which is Union of Beneficence being conducted at the highest speed from the highest variety, most diverse sources and this should be the thrust of knowledge for beneficial purposes. Here I would try to convey the spirit and essence of how we think things should be done. For example we should promote healthy competition but not unfair leg pulling. If someone is tall may be I am gifted in another way. So instead of cutting his legs we should develop a way to compliment mutual strength.

These few pages may have given the reader a comprehensive prelude into what is considered the most important aspect of human life's economic aspect which will convert mankind from a ferocious animal into a productive contributing human being.

In the following pages I will discuss some areas of economic activities that have been neglected and a great effort is needed to reach the desired optimum levels.

We would now like the reader to refer to our **Chapter 5(part 1): 62 Ways of Looting People**. This matter will be of great interest to all sundry. Now there is not a shadow of doubt that the principle method of organized looting of the people and depriving them is the institution of interest. The basic arguments which are put forward by the proponents of interest based economies are the following:

1. Interest creates capital
2. Interest compensates for inflation
3. Interest compensates for indexation
4. Interest compensates for devaluation
5. Interest compensates for equity and depreciation

Dear reader, we might smile a while because all these things are actually the same things which are artificial playing around with the price of things i.e. commodities and currencies. As per the natural law of economics which is the law number one of economics, there can be no increase in price.

This is the crux of the matter and when the readers read the statement of this law and rebuttal of the five above mentioned points raised in the favor of interest based diabolical system, and compares it with the law of expanding beneficence with increasing speed of circulation, it becomes crystal clear to the reader how the shortfall is compensated and over-come and the interest based economy is fully rebutted.;

P.S: Any shortfall which may remain due to human weakness and error of hoarding wealth or overspending (both of which are equally bad) can be removed by:

1 Taxation
2 Discouragement of consumerism

The practical way of achieving this will be to fix the price of 100-150 commodities all over the world.

Now we will come to second natural law of economics according to which every man is bound to increase beneficial things with hard honest and sensible work (details to follow).

GECOMETRA (GLOBAL ECONOMIC MANAGEMENT TECHNOLOGY and RESEARCH ORGANIZATION)

Economic development is closely related to the political situation and this has to be kept in mind. Consequently we will touch upon this matter here; as well as under **"POLITIKA"** in the following. Economic problems are the most serious problems facing humanity. Also refer to Chapter 1 (part 2) of this book.

This section will emphasize the production increase as well as progress with the principles of beneficence. It will also emphasize **supplemented economies**[3] with complete fairness and full political will of the people and leaders.

Mankind is in misery whether rich or poor. How can there be happiness in this terrible injustice. Believe me the accumulated economic injustice and malpractices have put man to a slow painful death; the greatest in history. The old injustices and horrors of war pale into insignificance compared to the slow and sure degeneration and degradation of economic deprivation and difficulty.

We have identified 13 different divisions and 92 subdivisions where work needs to be done. This is a roadmap for a government or a combination of governments and this is not a small project, and each one of these will require hundreds of specialists. UOB is a path for the whole world so at this stage, please do not feel overwhelmed, bored or impatient.

If you study the government structure you will see that many of these structures already exist under different names but they need a fresh start with entirely different motivation and creativity.

Please note that Health and Education are not included in **GECOMETRA** not because they are not important but we don't think they are money making areas and none of them is in complete isolation from the other.

Our approach is Patience and Perseverance, Disarmament-Armament, Give rather than Take, Circulate don't Stagnate, Use don't Lose, towards Beauty and Cleanliness, Earn by Producing not Plundering, Economic Man vs Economic Animal, Use what you have, Achieve more with less, Live and let live, We win-You win- the best situation.

---

[3]   Supplementing economies to the extent that healthy competition remains but the deadly competition will be eliminated and the existing economic system blends into the new system instead of clashing with it so that people wholeheartedly accept it and the new system will be at the same time adaptive to the good points of the old system; as we do not want to deprive ourselves of the old experiences and wisdom learnt over thousands of years- i.e. avoiding reinventing of the wheel.

4.1 AWE CLEAN–Clean Air, water and Environment:

We will work not only in cleaning the air and water from an environmentalist perspective - the common perception of clean environment, but also cleaning it from a social perspective. So that the life, honor and property of every individual is given full protection and the political environment is fair, just and conducive. So that individual interest and benefit is in line with the collective interest. We propose a middle ground wherein the interests and benefit of the individual and the collective society are in conformity instead of individual benefiting and the society being destroyed or the society benefiting and individual suffering.

4.2 ARIF -Agro Rashid Integrated Farms:

The food available to people is very low in quantity and quality (un-fresh, low in nutritive value and diseased). ARIF will work to improve affordability, availability and quality of food by using latest modern technologies in integrated farming. Now our food program will release the population of earth from the drudgery and time wastage in producing in many cases unhygienic and mal-nutritious food and we can form the granaries and meat dairy fruit vegetable oasis with large industrial complexes providing packed food fresh and tasty and cooked using technology and utilizing the human and financial resources in a correct and useful manner and using best quality food materials, catering methods, high tech treatment quality control production from all sorts of bacteria and viruses again at state of the art technology. What this will do is to generate employment, bring people together from all corners, remove hunger and malnutrition and at the same time release say of 2 billion women years for more productive activities. Specific projects and their brief description are:

4.2.1 Oilo (Palm Oil, Olive oil, etc.)

4.2.2 Instafeedo

4.2.3 Meato

4.2.4 Dairyo

4.2.5 Fisho

4.2.6 Fruito

4.2.7 Vego

4.2.8 Honeyo

4.2.9 Nutso

4.2.10 Green Houso

4.2.11 Suko (Supply Chain and Marketing)

4.2.12 Non Edible Products (wood, manure, leather hides, herbal products and medicine, poultry feed etc.)

4.2.13 Nuclear Desalination

4.3 Zeenat(Clothing):

Using value added oil[4] (special plastics), cotton, wool and other raw materials to provide clothing to the poor and deprived people especially those living in mountains, deserts, rainy areas and other extreme conditions and the disabled persons.
Specific projects and their brief description in Zeenat are:

4.3.1 Woolen and Cotton

4.3.2 Snow garments

4.3.3 Rain and Water Proof

2.3.4 Plastic

4.3.5 Antiviral and Antipollution

4.3.6 Safety wear

4.3.7 Air-conditioned clothing

---

[4]   so that the oil producing countries and companies feel happy but they should think of giving a respite to the poor people

4.4 Madina:

Using fast track, low cost, light weight, energy efficient, earthquake and flood resistant building technologies and effective town planning techniques (that provides protection against natural disasters, uninterrupted energy supply, communication systems, clean drinking water and employ waste management techniques (waste recycling) while ensuring application of principles of healthy community living in rural and urban areas.

Specific projects and their brief description in Madina are:

4.4.1 Nu Homes (Plastic homes)

4.4.2 Mega Polis (mega cities)

4.4.3 Real Estate (Consolidation, titles, acquisition, unification, development)

4.4.4 Town Planning (Dome compound), meeting places for different age groups, fire protection, safety and protection

4.4.5 Fuel efficient/ zero fuel HVAC (Heating, Ventilation and Air-conditioning)

4.5 RAZIA BIO-PHARMA:

4.5.1 Genetics (Stem Cell)

4.5.2 Pharma

4.5.3 Anti-Viral

4.6 TTTT- Transport Travel, Trade Terminal:

Specific projects and their brief description in TTTT are:

4.6.1 Transport

Nuclear Train, Ship
City Mass Navigation

4.6.2 Travel Passenger

4.6.3 Trade /Commercial Cargo

4.6.4 Terminals

4.7 NRE- Natural Resources and Environment:

Specific projects and their brief description in NRE are:

4.7.1 Land

4.7.2 Shores

4.7.3 Sea and Marines

4.7.4 Water, River and Lakes

4.7.5 Forests

4.7.6 Minerals

4.7.7 Dams

4.7.8 Air

4.7.9 Mountains

4.8 AKASH (Space):

Specific projects and their brief description in AKASH are:

4.8.1 Space Rocket Technology

4.8.2 Satellite Technology

4.8.3 Study of Time, Space and Electromagnetic Forces and Space Exploration

4.9 PEM-ENGG (Processes, Energy and Materials Engineering):

Specific projects and their brief description in PEM-ENGG are:

4.9.1 Defense

4.9.2 Electronics

4.9.3 Computers

4.9.4 Controls

4.9.5 Robotics

4.9.6 Non-Lethal Weapons

4.9.7 Communications

4.9.8 Metallurgy and Materials

4.9.9 Gravitronics

4.9.10 Mechatronics

4.9.11 Disarmament Armament

4.9.12 Industrial Engineering

4.9.13 Consumer Products

4.9.14 Information Technology

4.9.15 Energy

    4.9.15.1 Geothermal

    4.9.15.2 Electric

    4.9.15.3 Nuclear

4.9.15.4 Hydal

4.9.15.5 Tidal

4.9.15.6 Solar

4.9.15.7 Wind

4.9.15.8 Hydrogen/Fuel Cell

4.9.16 Processes

4.9.17 Chemicals

4.9.18 Hardware and Software

4.10 CORECO (COORDINATION AND REFORM COUNCIL):

Specific projects and their brief description in CORECO are:

4.10.1 Private Business Chambers

4.10.2 Government Agencies

4.10.3 Academic Research

4.10.4 Training Institutes

4.10.5 Chartered Accountants

4.10.6 Banks

4.10.7 Regulatory and Legal Bodies

4.10.8 Cooperatives

4.11 ORIMMSSA-DM Operations Research Interdisciplinary Mathematical Modeling Solutions Synthesis Analysis and Decision Making:

Specific projects and their brief description in ORIMMSSA are:

4.11.1 Beneficence Operations Research

4.11.2 Interdisciplinary

4.11.3 Mathematical

4.11.4 Modeling

4.11.5 Solutions

4.11.6 Synthesis

4.11.7 Analysis and Decision Making

4.12 UVUV Finance, Trade and Marketing (Interest free):

The basic principle is UV (you- we) as against VVV (we, we, we) as you know. Agreement system, growth through supplemental assets.

Specific projects and their brief description in UVUV are:

4.12.1 Finance, Financing, E-Finance and Funds

4.12.2 Banking (Interest Free)

4.12.3 Exchange

4.12.4 Securities

2.11.5 Holdings

4.12.6 Leasing

4.12.7 Stocks

4.12.8 Islamic Financing: Modaraba, Musharaka, Murabiha, Ijara, Takaaful

4.12.9 Mutual Funds, REITS

4.12.10 Trade and Investments (Metals and commodities), ebay

4.12.11 Marketing, Whole Selling, Retailing, Super Markets

4.13 World Human Resource and Development Fund:

4.13.1 Commercial Education and Trainings

4.13.2 Immigration, Human Capital Export, Indigenous with Skills and Language of host countries

4.13.3 Computerized Mathematical Calculation of Zakat in an Accurate Manner using one year condition

4.13.4 Courts of Economic Crimes Against Humanity.

CHAPTER 5
UOB Division Three

POLITIKA-OVER ALL MANAGEMENT OF HUMAN AFFAIRS

Prior to talking in detail about *'POLITIKA'*, as we have mentioned that politics is the sum total of human knowledge related to management of human affairs as a whole. So it is the determining factor of how society will run in all individual and collective aspects of life.

The reader will at once feel that POLITIKA includes aspects of economics, technology, Achademia and they are all overlapping and interlinked, but this should not confuse the reader at all. The reality is that human life is one integrated whole, where one part is sometimes emphasized and another part at some other time. Practically we are emphasizing our resources and energies to one aspect and sometimes to another while trying to do so rather unsuccessfully because of the frailty of human nature and limitation of his capacities, which is not usually harmoniously functioning like a well-ousted and well balanced machine. This is in the nature of things as they are and though we can try to make efforts to the contrary but human efforts are never perfect.

The second reason for this is the way our mental faculties work. Man likes to classify things into different compartments, so that he can make sense at of the rigmarole and confusion around him. The better and more detailed the classification the more it appears that there is a grasp over the situation but alas the frailties inherent in human affairs, this is at some loss of adaptability and fluidity. So the cycle of life goes on, like a transition of an amoeba with no shape to a rigid bone like structure.

Nevertheless there is a consensus and consensus means a lot, that the political affairs and the affairs in general are very deeply and extensively related to the economic aspect of life, which is the fulfillment of man's material requirement (we will not attempt to burden the reader as it has been already discussed earlier that how much these needs matter and how much energy they require). A person may need a smile but that calls for energy. In the divine books this is simplified as the expenditure of wealth and life. What is life? Life is will, life is motivation, life is growth and reproduction and life is your social and value system. Let me explain it with an example. You may give a hundred pounds in charity, but you may throw it with disdain or you may give it nicely.

Having said this, we have mentioned the general consensus on the importance of economic matters; wealth and life, energy resources, material etc. With the passage of time man has acquired more and more control over the communication means. May I dare to say that communication is life itself! This has come with the development of technology and it would not be wrong to say that technology has acquired more and more importance in politics. (What an amazing statement!) The computerized data, the role of media, the global village, the integration and interdependence of human society speaks volume about what we have said.

Now we will jump again from the pure philosophical to the very practical, without which this write-up would be nothing but a philosophical treatise. In my humble opinion, no! I should perhaps put it in a question form. Who is the most important person in society today? Is he the media man or the politician, the military general or the artist? Is he the judge or the businessman, the lawyer or the bureaucrat or the teacher? You will be surprised when I would say NO, none of these! He is the **engineer** and the **scientist** and the **linguist** and the **information expert**. Although I know I should throw a lot of light on this statement, but at this stage I would leave it to the reader, if he can evaluate the validity of this statement critically, whereas I will attempt to explain it later.

We have seen that that the corrupt system of politicians, judges, population welfare workers, teacher trainers, to a lesser extent media and military men, railway department, all the ministries and municipalities are run through taking loans by IMF or World Bank, which are re-paid in the form of utility bills, fares, taxes, raising fuel prices etc. All these funds go into the pocket of corrupt people and common man has to foot the bill. So the main tool which makes it possible is the engineers like civil and electrical engineers working in electric supply companies, construction, heavy industries etc. and technologists in the field of agriculture science (not subject to this kind of corruption). It is a vicious cycle which has brought the world to a grinding halt.

Now coming to the reconstruction of the world political system, what we will need is a surprise of the surprises. We need to develop a new breed of scientists, engineers etc. To do this, we have to make sacrifices of many of our present engineers, scientists etc. at the altar of betterment of humanity.

The first step in this regard will be what we call CLEAN and DEVELOP, by eliminating perhaps not by bloodshed but by replacement and disposal of the corrupt elements within each one of the important category of professions-**ESLM²BATLR**.

The CLEAN process will start with cleaning of thoughts followed by corrective measures.

It is in the nature of human beings that crime should go with punishment and good deeds with rewards. Those people who are guilty of financial crimes (cruel leaders, corrupt officials, bankers, cons) are hunt mostly by taking away and confiscating their wealth. Similarly SQUARE RELEASE will focus on eradicating sectarianism, nationalism, inefficiency and all those aspects which lead to strife and discord (Fasad-fil-Arz). Remember Shylock Merchant of Venice. Those guilty of bloodshed should be beheaded i.e. their heads should be chopped off, while those who commit torture and mutilation should be treated accordingly to what they have done. "As you sow so shall you reap".

Another effect of this negative process is that increase in production in the various areas of GECOMETRA is not possible because people are not working! Hence chances of production are reduced by both corruption and inefficiency.

In the case of POLITIKA, I would like to request my readers to allow me to discuss it in the light of a case study of my notorious country Pakistan, which would be of interest otherwise also.

Regarding the political situation in Pakistan, one always thinks that what are the reasons for this debacle? Reasons are numerous but the major contributor after Ayub Khan and Sikander Mirza established dictatorship, was the so called civil-Chief Marshal Law administrator who with his diabolical ways, evil talent, considerable courage and mastery over Machiavellian politics destroyed all institutions in Pakistan after breaking it up by rejecting Sheikh Mujeeb-ur-Rehman- the majority leader from the then East Pakistan. Since the day he took over right up to today, even though he was brutally hanged and every single member of his family was killed sometimes by others and sometime by themselves (like Murtaza Bhutto's shooting by Benazir Bhutto). Such deep rooted foundations of mischief and strife through the American plan of taking over Afghanistan by using the so called Mujahidin makes everything very evident and we may not go into further detail about it. Period neither are they so important but for creating a menace amongst people so they can safeguard themselves and the country in future. Please note that Bhutto and his clan were representing the so called Shia minority to an extent where he took direct orders from Shah Iran who was the CIA thug in this region.

As for the economic problems of Pakistan this is the responsibility primarily amongst the many other relatively minor reasons, the Nawaz Sharif and Shahbaz Sharif gang who have looted Pakistan with cronies like Ishaq Dar and Mansha that even the so called evil political genius *Chotali Chakia* and Machiavelli will lower their heads in shame and bow before them with great respect.

Add to this the wonderful judicial system, the legacy of the British Empire who did everything to protect the injustice and the corrupt and punish the honest and delay and deny the justice without an iota of doubt. Add to this wonderful Russian salad, a topping of blasted nationalist saleable or purchasable sectarian Mullahs and a garnish of seculars and communists. You need not to dwell further into the evils of our country.

What is the solution? The solution is to create awareness amongst the mainstream population in which the infamous media will play the role but it will be self-generated phenomena. Let me assure you with all the emphasis in my command that no power can stop this process of reform. Do what they may and it has already begun. Not to fizzle out and lead astray this time. Rest assure, O enemies of Islam and Pakistan, who challenged you, we the willing would do the impossible for the ungrateful. A challenge anybody to have a DO; DO Hath with us! Hip Hip Hurray.

The political system in Pakistan will comprise of the President of Pakistan who will be directly elected by the total population of Pakistan. There will be four federal Ministers: Minister of each of ACHADEMIA, GECOMETRA, POLITIKA and ASSOCIA. In the interim period of five years, the present Federal Ministries may work and slowly merge into the above format. President and Ministers will be scrutinized over a five year period through the media, investigative journalism, all agencies of the establishment and systematic information from Banks, FBR, NAB, Police, FIA, ECP and Judiciary through a well announced plan of scrutiny and counter verification of the Army. The Judiciary of Pakistan will comprise of only those judges who in addition to Law Degree will pass the *Faqih* exam to be granted by the council of Ulema-e-Haq. All political entities will transform into Hunafa Alliance for government and the Ihtisaab (accountability) Alliance for check and balance in a three tired structured. The word party will be banned in Pakistan and only the word League or Alliance could be used. The main league will be the AMAL league which under Hunafa Alliance can collaborate with other leagues which may be formed. The great struggle movement, "JUHD UL KUBRA" will be essentially the non-violence, non-cooperation, civil disobedience, democratic movement under the 1973 constitution comprising of 36000 ten mile grid centers, which will comprise of all good and capable people from nearly 50 walks and categories of life and professions. The vanguard of this *JuhdulGhaleeza* (in the words of Holy Quran) will be the propagation of Holy Quran itself.

This will immediately impose the *Shariah* (whether the non-Muslims like it or not) according to the modern requirements and abolish interest by 2018. The guideline, practical collaborations, standing order procedures and manuals will be formulated on top priority basis with utmost wisdom in the light of Quran, Hadith, Sunnah, Science, Technology, History and Current Affairs.

This will be concurrently working with special core of GECOMETRA and MI Telecom for fulfilling the economic requirements in next 5 years. All the good points of all the existing political systems will be taken into consideration through close study of governments and practices in other countries especially at procedural level. Emphasis will be on creative problem solving and practice of social and cultural norms. We want a principled and disciplined society but we want practical applications and productive solutions. We want information, action and application oriented society which is flexible with adaptive rules methods, techniques and procedures.

Finally since the system is being changed, the public will have to get familiarized with the new terminologies and discard the old ones such as:

> 'Information House'
> 'Intellectual factor'
> 'Think Tank'
> 'Issues, Problems and Solutions'
> 'Idea Factory'
> 'Computer Modeling'
> 'Decision Making'
> 'Interdisciplinary Operational Research'
> 'E-Govt.'

P.S. Practically it will be a three tiered arrangement, Local Government, Middle Government and National Government. The leadership will be selected on the law of natural selection from **ESLM²BATLR**.

National Interface Hunafa-Alliance Beneficence/ Amal League

The national level representation of Hunafa Alliance (which as mentioned earlier will be a league of political entities agreeing on the principles of beneficence) will be through the Beneficence/Amal Party.

Manifesto:

1. This party has not come to make promises but to take promises and to punish the criminals, which can go up to death penalty. Financial corruption and looting the public wealth will be eradicated and punishable by capital punishments. (Previous criminals can redeem themselves by returning the looted wealth or by paying compensation including financial penalty). Government employees and representatives will not be allowed to misuse national wealth/ property in any case and violators will be strictly punished incrementally. All the people the looters, bankers, sectarians, nationalist and Communist groups will be given six years notice of execution whereas incompetent people will be made to work.

2. The government will ensure maintaining of law and order; Protection of life, honor and property; Provision of basic necessities like clean drinking water, food, health care utilities etc.

3. Violence, riots, destruction of public property for resolving issues will not be allowed in any case. No linguistic, ethnic or sectarian activity will be allowed.

4. All affairs of state and society will be run on the system of justice and consultation. Justice department, Education department, Minerals department, Natural resource department, trade department, Financial department, Customs etc. will be completely revamped.

5. Mainstream development of democracy and mobilization of Civil Society at mega interactivity and connectivity as a principle. We believe in democracy, devolution and free flow of ideas as well as continuous evolution /improvement in the democratic system solutions, re-introduction of local government in modified form, information in an interactive and integrative method using latest communication techniques and technologies starting from convergent media, digital and social media, viral marketing in multilingual formats.

6. Manpower and human resource will be developed for both domestic and export purposes. Those not complying will be handed over to the government for forced labor.

7. Those going abroad and want to keep Pakistani citizenship will be required to pay additional taxes. Deductions will be made from the money they send to Pakistan for Government and the Parents.

8. CARE: Government and the Society will be responsible for taking care of the old, weak, needy, orphans, poor, sick, crippled and those in distress. For this dedicated staff at every union council will monitor their area and maintain authentic and updated records. Elder citizens will be given blue passports and young will support the old especially, daughters and sons.

9. Beneficence - Munificence (abundant wealth): Both the government and the citizens will be responsible for increasing legitimate national wealth more than the increase in population by increasing productivity. Cyclic Theory of Economics vs. Reciprocating Theory of Economics.

10. Interest will be abandoned fully and immediately. Abolition of State banks and strict scrutiny of all the money going out of the country.

11. A balanced, unanimous, and most advanced education system and media based on Quran, Sunnah/Hadith, Science and modern Social Sciences and arts will be developed and implemented. Arrangements will be made to teach Vocational Skills for the Emancipation of Poor.

Note 1: A unanimous agreement by leaders of different sects, areas, geographic and ethnic groups, leading religious and modern scholars and spiritual leaders will be reached in this regard.

Note 2: All non-Muslims will be allowed to get education in accordance with their beliefs and they will have complete freedom, legal and financial protection, indiscriminate representation and employment opportunities in businesses and employment (except for in armed forces and constitutional and key sensitive posts).

The salient features of this education system will be as follows:

a) Compulsory education will be for a maximum duration of 14 years.
b) **Youth Incentive & Utilization Program-YIP (18-50 years).**
c) Every educated person will be provided employment by the government worth at least Rs.10, 000/ per month.
d) Parents Compensation Program PCP (above 50 years).
e) The government will pay Rs.1 million in compensation to every parent whose child has completed 16 years of compulsory education except in case of family business in which the child works. The child will pay Rs.0.5 million extra to his/her parents on completion of each higher education degree or work in lieu of the amount payable.
f) Every citizen will give his /her annual productivity report to the government.
g) Adult education program.
h) Education of human relations.
i) Arrangement of spiritual education and eradicating jealousy and rivalry while promoting healthy completion.

12. **Mega polis revival:** There is shortage of 8 million houses in Pakistan. Housing department will provide weather proof, calamity proof construction to every family.
13. Release and Utilization of Natural Resources.
14. Creativity and innovation will be encouraged.
15. Converting Pakistan into Multimillion Multilingual THE LANGUAGE COUNTRY. This will include Human Resource Development of Languages (HRDL); 500,000 trained persons in each language. WOLAM-IMPEX; Woman Language Man Mass Import Export
16. Early rising and early start of work day

17. Termination of all civil engineers. Most of the problems in our services and infrastructure which have made life miserable for the people are due to the incompetence and corruption of civil engineers. Water and sanitation, sewage and drainage, housing and buildings, dams, irrigation and canals, roads and passages, bridges, urban master planning and municipal administration all are in shambles. The old system has to be abolished and reconstituted by establishment of Pakistan Civil Council in addition to the existing PEC. This council will undertake reconstruction/ rehabilitation/ rectification of dangerous and faulty structures, buildings and designs.

18. We want to mobilize the goodness and talents, development of thought, language and techniques, spend less on self and more on others *Al-Afu, e.g.* medical services are too expensive so we introduce preventive medicine, health exercise and cleanliness, hygiene including bio chemic, Tibb-e-Nabawi and Quran.

19. A green Pakistan using canals, rivers, Nuclear Desalination Plants and REVIRS (reverse rivers).Turning Pakistan into food basket for the region.

20. Civil defense and security.

21. IKEM 25.

22. KKK-Character, Knowledge and Capability.

23. Recreation, Arts and Culture.

24. Development of political and historical awareness.

25. Editorial board to work on family manual (monthly magazines e.g. Kiran, Shuaa and Khwateen) and Guidance Manuals 'The Package' in other fields.

26. MILEX: Military Export, Peacekeeping force under US command or any other human control.

27. Division of provinces into equitable shapes such as the S.

28. SAFE Country watch.

Membership:

The membership of Beneficence Amal League will be subject to oath of allegiance to the manifesto, which will be as follows:

Oath of Allegiance:

- Promise to be truthful
- Promise to be honest
- Promise to be hardworking
- Promise to be competent

- Promise not be prejudiced
- Promise not to create mischief

Leadership:

The leadership will be selected on the law of natural selection, from ESLAM²BTLR and impeccably honest, selfless, capable, creative and productive (making most out of the least). Spiritual Testing will be employed and people will be branded accordingly; Leadership will be representing every section of the society in three – four vertical tires and it will have two horizontal tires each showing mirror of the other as the mirror reflects the mistakes and good points. There is 51 % chance of mistake of one, whereas one in a billion of that of two, keeping the same 70 % accuracy of source information but with different roots (Operational Research in decisions and control by Stafford Bear ORISMA). A new cadre of leadership will be born i.e. a joint integrated, political, economic, social and spiritual leadership inspired by clear goals of beneficence service, brilliance, character and truthfulness.

Structure: Grand National Council- The Ten Mile Grid

The total area of Pakistan is 365000 sq. miles. Dividing it into a 10 square mile grid, gives us 3650 geographical clusters. A group of 20 core members belonging to different professions will be formed within each cluster. Hence, a total of 3650 clusters will be formed with an average of 10 cluster groups per tehsil having a total of 73000 core members. Each cluster will have a 5 year's tenure. The 73000 core members will form the Grand National Council of the Beneficence Amal League.

Beneficence Amal League 10 point plan

1) Political diversification and integration.
2) Management and administrative reforms based on justice, thankfulness, and public interest.
3) Parents compensation plan.
4) Brain drain and brawn drain.
5) Development and protection of natural resources.
6) Human resource development – policies and goals.
7) Bureaucrats, customs, forest minerals, water banks, and financial institution reforms.
8) Food, Housing, Health and Education reforms.
9) Spiritual and ethical development.

10) Social development.
11) Nishtar/ Clean.
12) Constitutional reforms.

Methods:

- 350 Tehsil Conventions (20 professionals 7 for, 7 neutral, 6 against), (in approximately 50 professions).
- 135 District Conventions.
- 7 Provincial Conventions
- 10 International Mega Conventions
    - National and International conferences in Pakistan; The Hub of Future.
    - Convention Centers
    - Display and Address Centers AV Shows.

Beneficence Party Center: Refer to Chart 1

Multinational and Regional Interface: GRB

We want to suggest a century breaking idea:

We the people of Pakistan do hereby invite the most senior and mutually accepted government and public representatives from all countries to sit in along with the representatives of all the unrepresented organs and segments of our state to form the Regional Congress of Representatives, like the Judiciary, Police, Government and the Middle class in the third house of parliament, and reciprocally representatives of our country will represent in other countries. And they will have very significant vote of Yes or No in slowly evolving legislation, policies, plans and this will lay the foundation of the Global Regional Blocks.

Let us look at Chart 6

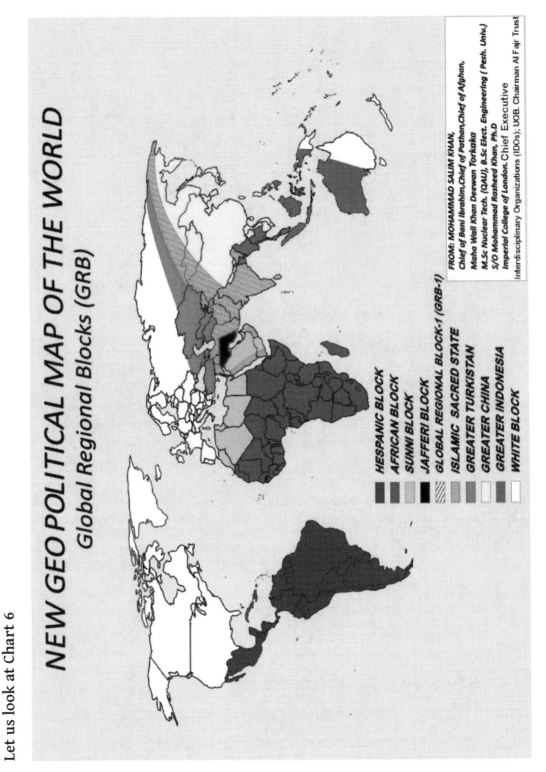

NEW GEO POLITICAL MAP OF THE WORLD
Global Regional Blocks (GRB)

HESPANIC BLOCK
AFRICAN BLOCK
SUNNI BLOCK
JAFFERI BLOCK
GLOBAL REGIONAL BLOCK-1 (GRB-1)
ISLAMIC SACRED STATE
GREATER TURKISTAN
GREATER CHINA
GREATER INDONESIA
WHITE BLOCK

FROM: MOHAMMAD SALIM KHAN,
Chief of Bani Ibrahim,Chief of Pathan,Chief of Afghan,
Maha Wali Khan Deerwan Torkaka
M.Sc Nuclear Tech. (QAU), B.Sc Elect. Engineering (Pesh. Univ.)
S/O Mohammad Rasheed Khan, Ph.D
Imperial College of London. Chief Executive
interdisciplinary Organizations (IDOs); UOB. Chairman Al Fajr Trust

The second aspect of POLITIKA is related to ideology. These are often opposing each other and cause the political struggle.

After talking in detail about POLITIKA, as we have mentioned that Politics is the management of human affairs so it is the determining factor of how society will run in all individual and collective aspects of life. It is an established principle that there is no compulsion or coercion in a person's or society's selection of the way of life. Having said that we are proposing a charter or a manifesto of a way of life which we think is suitable. In this matter it may not be regarded as if we are trying to impose our thoughts. As said in the Quran:

"There is no compulsion in Faith" (Al Baqarah; V: 256)

But of course one should be ready for the consequences of the way of life he or a group or a nation chooses.

"For you is your faith, and for me, my faith." (Al Kafirun; V: 6)

So in this way we are really giving the practical example of Unity and Diversity i.e. the accommodation of various groups to bear with the differences while at the same time unite in thought and deed where they agree. And we are saying it openly as again it is the spirit of Union of Beneficence not to hide the common. In the charter of Union of Beneficence, there is no chance of covert action.

Let us take the case of an Islamic country X. It may evolve a charter as given below:

Truly, the (recognized) religion in the sight of Allah is Islam. (Al Imran; V: 19)

Declaration of "The United States of Islam"

Verily and surely the Religion (by which is meant the way of life) is definitely and only Islam (Al Quran)

The purpose of this declaration is to call towards Islam in a comprehensive and clear manner based on which we, Muslims will collectively and with singleness of purpose, lay the foundation of "The United States of Islam"-Insha Allah.

Important Explanation:

This declaration is based on verses of the Holy Quran and sayings of the Holy Prophet (PBUH).

Open Invitation (The message of acting upon Islam)

People belonging to all areas, professions and strata of society are invited to make a pledge today that we will identify our weaknesses and mistakes, try our best to rectify our hearts, thoughts and deeds, collectively repent and seek Allah's blessings, forgiveness and help. We are suffering from numerous types of social and economic problems, disgrace and pain as punishment of our deeds. The path to salvation is only this.

> *Surely, Allah does not change the condition of a people unless they change themselves. (Al Raad; V: 11)*

Allah is giving us the opportunity to change ourselves again and again. The Muslim Nation as a whole has fallen into the depths of humiliation and disgrace. If we don't take practical and truthful steps to change our circumstances now, it might get too late. If we continue with our gaiety and rebellious attitude, then a terrible end is inevitable. Bosnia, Kashmir, Afghanistan and Palestine examples from all over the world are in front of us. May Allah protect Pakistan! (Ameen!)

This country which was built in the name of Islam is sore in the eyes of the people who hate Islam in spite of our good wishes for them. We have been divided into groups and entangled in political, economic, cultural and technical problems. Our capabilities have been paralyzed. We have to collectively counter the enemy's conspiracy. We have to guard this fort of Islam. Our Religion is one, Quran is one, Prophet (PBUH) one - then why dispute amongst ourselves and remain divided?

Collective Repentance

Let us remove our differences and present before our Creator and our Lord and pray to Him in a humble manner and reform ourselves according to His way. Let us repent collectively and sincerely, revive our Faith and embrace Islam in our individual and collective lives for eternal success. Allah rewards those who repent, are true believers, fear Him and perform good deeds; both in this world and in the hereinafter.

Revival of Faith

Let us all together, fearing Almighty Allah, truthfully and firmly recognize ourselves as Muslims. Let us bear witness with full consciousness, in our heart and with our tongue that "There is no God but Allah and Muhammad is His messenger." It is our belief that;

- ***There is none worthy of worship except Allah. He is One and He has no partner with Him.*** We will only worship Him and will do so willingly. Sovereignty and supreme authority is for Him only. The decision of good and bad, permissible and forbidden is only His. He is our Creator and our Master- *Rehman* and *Raheem*. Sustainer of the worlds. All praise is for Him. He is free from all faults and weaknesses. He is All Knowing and All Seeing. He is Omnipotent and all matters are decided by Him only. He begets not nor was begotten.

He is Strong and Patient. We will have our trust in Him and seek help from Him only. Whatever is there in the skies and in the worlds is His and we will worship only Him, Love Him and join no one with Him. All beautiful names are for Him and no one is like Him.

• The **Second part of our faith** is that Prophet Muhammad (PBUH) is the Last Prophet and Messenger of Allah. The Prophet (PBUH) is mercy for all the worlds. He is the last Messenger of Allah for all the worlds. Annunciation of the Holy Prophet (PBUH) is above the domain of time and space and nation and language. His life is the best role model and a beacon for us. Following his ways, his sunnah and his sayings is obligatory for us.

Only in this way we can lead the straight path and seek salvation and success. After Allah, we love the Prophet (PBUH) and we will always keep sending our blessings on him. We also believe in all previous prophets of Allah, but Mohammad (PBUH) is the last and the leader of all the Prophets – who has brought the complete way of life from Allah.

• The **Third part of our faith** is the Holy Quran which is the last divine Book from Allah. Allah revealed it to the heart of our beloved Prophet (PBUH) through the Angel Gabriel Amin in the form of *"Wahi"* divine revelation. Allah has taken the responsibility to protect the Holy Quran and to spread its message. No one can change it and no other book can be like it. It is the Word of Allah. It is the criterion for the right and the wrong, the good and the evil and is very blessed *Furqan-e-Majeed* (distinguishing truth from falsehood). It is a source of guidance for those who believe in the unseen, who fear Allah, who believe in Allah's prophets, who believe in the hereafter, establish Prayer and give Zakat (Alms). It leads us to that straight path which the Prophet (PBUH) followed- which leads towards Allah and towards *Jannah/* Paradise i.e. towards the real and eternal success. It is a light and cure for hearts. Its reading, understanding and acting upon it, is obligatory for us. Spreading its teachings in a good and sincere manner is a prime duty for us. The fate of nations is decided upon how strongly they hold on to The Holy Quran. This is the rope of Allah which joins us with Him, with His Prophet (PBUH) and with true Muslims.

- The **Fourth part of our faith is to believe in *life after death***. The day of resurrection, the Day of Judgment, reward and punishment, life after death, *Jannah*/Paradise and *Jahannam*/Hell are all indisputable. The real success is of the life after death. This world is the playing field for *Hereafter*. Each one of us has to go from this transitory world and face death. This world is an examination room and a mere game and show for those who do not understand its reality. Everyone has to go and present him/herself one by one on the day of resurrection – which will be the Day of Judgment and reward and punishment. On that day the final rule will be purely for Allah alone. He who submitted and did good deeds (which Allah accepted with His mercy) will be rewarded with Jannah/Paradise. He who denied, ascribed partners or rivals to Allah, did hypocrisy and disobeyed, then insisted upon it and stood in revolt against Allah and his Prophet (PBUH) till his last breath, then surely Hell will be his final abode (except if he repents before death/the last breath and act righteously).

- The **Fifth part of our faith** is to believe in the Angels of Allah; that they are incontrovertible and they keep praising Allah all the time and run the system of the universe for man as per instructions of Allah. They do not err one bit in doing so. They do not have a choice of their own. They have been created from light and are pure from all sins. They all bowed down in front of Adam following Allah's order.

- The **Sixth part of our faith is to believe in fate**. We accept that all good and bad circumstances are from Allah Almighty. A Muslim is not affected by external circumstances. He always remains obedient and thankful to Allah, remains His humble and patient servant, always turning towards Him and seeking help from Him. He embraces all circumstances (good or bad) and duties happily in order to seek Allah's pleasure and keeps on doing good deeds. Allah always has mercy on man. Bad circumstances are a result of one's own deeds.

The Fight between Good and Evil- Man and Satan

Allah has created man for His worship. He is the best among His creations. Allah gave him the best shape, the ability to think, understand and to speak. Allah gave him knowledge. Then showed him the right and the wrong path and took promise of His worship from all human beings even before their birth. Allah created man from soil and put His soul in him and appointed him His vicegerent on earth and ordered the angels to bow in front of him. Whatever is there in this world, Allah has subdued for him. Allah created all the humans from the couple of Adam and Eve. Allah gave man the ability to do right or wrong, emotions, thought, knowledge, wisdom and free will to a certain extent. He put both good and evil in him. Then gave him life and death, so that he can be tested in his actions. Also told him that man will get what he struggles for. Good in return for good and evil in return for evil.

Satan (*Iblees*) was from amongst the Jinns (created from fire with limited will). He refused to bow to Adam despite of Allah's command due to his pride and jealousy, and was expelled from Allah's proximity. He became a symbol of hopelessness, anger, pride, jealousy and breaking of relationships. He is man's biggest enemy. He obtained permission to lead human beings astray till the day of resurrection. He is man's biggest and most dangerous enemy. He inclines man towards greed, false hopes, deceit, love of wealth, wrong desires, pride, jealousy, grudge, hatred, disunity, lies, mischief, misery and even ascribing rivals to Allah.

He misleads people though temptation, and destroys their life in this world and in the hereafter. It is our duty that we save ourselves completely from his armies. It is our duty to save ourselves from Satan and his forces. We will fight him through reading Quran, remembrance of Allah (*dhikar*), sending blessings to the Prophet (PBUH), offering prayers, giving alms, showing kindness towards one another, sincerity, wisdom and knowledge, good intentions and righteous deeds and consider him our biggest enemy. We will save ourselves, our families and other fellow Muslims from him. His tricks fail to work on sincere servants of Allah.

Fundamental Principles and Objectives

- Worshiping Allah happily will be our duty and objective and the primary **Purpose** of our life.
- Establishing **Allah's Caliphate** in this world, bearing witness to the truth and establishing the religion-Islam will be our primary activity.
- Cooperation in good deeds; enjoining what is right and forbidding what is wrong will be our way.
- Our friendship and enmity will be for Allah's sake only and we are displeased and disgusted/annoyed with the way of Christians, Jews, Polytheist, transgressors and hypocrites.
- Our guardian is Allah, His Prophet (PBUH) and the believers who establish prayers, remain united, give Zakat and obey Allah and His Messenger (PBUH).
- We will avoid discord amongst ourselves.
- We will decide matters through **Shura** i.e. mutual consultation and give important responsibilities only to capable people.
- We will maintain balance in our spiritual, academic, practical and collective affairs.

- "Sincerity, Knowledge and Faith", "Piety, Justice and Welfare", "Brotherhood, Discipline and Unity", "Worship of Allah and Service of His creation" will be our guiding principles.

Fields of Action

Man can have nothing but what he strives for. Faith cannot be complete without good actions and manners and without this we cannot seek salvation in the hereafter. Action is necessary with Faith. Only sincere action based on Knowledge and Wisdom is acceptable to Allah and will be rewarded by Him in the hereafter.

Therefore we pledge that we will adopt our lives both individually and collectively as per Quran and Sunnah - trusting Allah, maintaining unity of the Ummah/Nation, struggling by spending our wealth and bodies, being aware of what is permitted and what is forbidden, demonstrating steadfastness, good manners, patience and thankfulness, being fully prepared, willingly, having good intentions and love for Allah, His Prophet (PBUH) and the believers, repenting, keeping balance, seeking Allah's pleasure, for the success of *Akhira* and for entering into paradise, struggling all the time with full force in all realms of life.

More details of this is as follows:

1. Establishing individual and collective system of worship

- ➤ We will establish the system of **_Salah_** i.e. prayers. This will be given primary importance. Neighborhood and Central Mosques will be the centers of lives of Muslims. Promoting discord and other un-Islamic acts will not be permitted in them.
- ➤ Proper system for payment of Zakat, alms, Ushr and Khums (for whom it is compulsory) will be established with full honesty and trustworthiness.
- ➤ Proper arrangements will be made for fasting in the month of Ramadan (for whom it is compulsory).
- ➤ Proper arrangements will be made for performing Hajj (for whom it is compulsory).

2. Education, Propagation and calling towards of Islam

We pledge to adapt our education system according to Quran and Sunnah. Instead of promoting materialism through our education system, we will promote traits like seeking pleasure of Allah, following the Prophet (PBUH) and striving for success of the hereafter. Secularism and other such factors will be removed from the education system, courses and books in an effective and wise manner. Co-education will be completely abolished. Quality Islamic schools, colleges and universities will be promoted. This will include research organizations.

The **criteria and method of education** will be cleansed from 'economic greed.' Islamic civilization, manners, self-confidence, alertness, piety, creativity, research and other such qualities will be promoted among teachers and students instead of western culture and civilization. The concept of 'education for livelihood' will be balanced out and superior objectives of getting education will be given importance.

Education in Science, History, Linguistics and other worldly fields of knowledge will be arranged in a much better way and a proper balance maintained between religious and worldly knowledge. Cheating and dishonesty in exams will be strictly prohibited.

Islamic and Arabic courses will be stared in homes, neighborhoods and mosques.

Education in **Quran and Sunnah** and other fields of beneficial knowledge will be made cheap and easy. More and more advanced and reliable means and resources will be used for **mass broad-cast and publicity** and propagation. Big, deep and long lasting practical changes will be brought in the field of education.

3. Society, Ethics and Culture:

In this way we will promote our social, ethical and cultural lives on the basis of Quran, Sunnah and virtue. We will adapt our way of living, clothing, timings, rituals, relationships, marriages, greetings, meetings and social gatherings, birth and death, condolences, worships, attendance of sick, festivals and sports according to the principles of Islam.

We will uproot immodesties. Absurd and useless acts like smoking, gambling, cinema, playing cards will be discouraged. Instead attractive and beautiful ways of entertainment based on modesty and cleanliness will be promoted.

We will encourage respect of women, chastity, kindness to the young and respect of elders, leniency with workers, kindness with relatives and other fellow Muslims, good manners and actions, seeking well-being of others and serving others. The sick, poor and needy, disadvantaged, orphans, widows and the old will be taken special care of and arrangements for serving them will be made.

All disliked actions and behaviors that lead towards strife or discord like lies, embezzlement, back biting, making false accusations, bad manners, miserliness, holding grudge, baseless animosity etc. will be finished through *training* so that a virtuous/ righteous society can be established.

We will protect every Muslim's life, property and honor at the societal level. Similarly all efforts will be made to finish unhealthy thinking based on pride, jealousy, thanklessness, greed and selfishness. Environment, homes and settlements will be built on Islamic lines.

4. Justice and Law:

We will decide our legal matters i.e. life, property and honor disputes according to the Islamic Law- Shariah. The Police, court, patwari, judges and lawyers system established by the British will have to adapt according to Islamic principles. Until then, this system will be boycotted and alternate system will be established in which Scholars, Islamic legal/jurisprudence experts and Jirga system will be used for decision making.

Convicts will be punished in time, in a fair and just manner on the basis of truth and it will be ensured that everyone is equal in the eyes of law.

We will witness truthfully and help the victims. Every Muslim's life, property and honor will be protected and will be forbidden for other Muslim.

No one will be permitted to look down or ridicule another. Cruelty by individual or by state will be eliminated.

A fair and just system of accountability, reward and punishment will be established and capable and honest people will be entrusted with the responsibility. Departments of Police and Justice will be completely restructured. Evil will be eliminated and good ordained.

5. Economic Life and economics

We will align our economic system with Quran and Sunnah. National Wealth will be kept into a state of circulation and production as much as possible. The wealth which Allah has placed in earth will be fully utilized and used in a just manner. All actions will be taken with complete honesty, frugality, efficiency, in a well-planned, disciplined and sequenced manner.

All forbidden acts like interest, bribery, dishonesty, theft, storage, usurping, and wager will be completely banned.

All types of interest based transactions will be completely boycotted. These will be finished and replaced with alternate systems of Dar-ul-Mal, Bait-ul-Mal and wealth committees.

Economic development and natural resources will be utilized and distributed in the best possible and just manner. We will earn Halal income for ourselves and our families with hard work and honesty through permitted businesses, agriculture, industry and handicrafts, mining etc. Extreme concentration of capital / wealth-the biggest cause of which is interest will be completely eliminated. Additional wealth will be taken from the rich and distributed among the poor, the disadvantaged, the widows, orphans, travelers, needy and the deserving. This wealth will be utilized in service of mankind, in addressing national needs and for collective welfare.

Simple living will be adopted and miserliness and extravagance will be refrained from. Frugality will be adopted and resources will be best utilized. National wealth will be utilized as per the Islamic way. Similarly inflation, unemployment and economic injustice will be eliminated. National economy will be completely relieved of debts and Jewish institutions.

6. Government employees and Professionals

Every person will follow special Islamic teachings according to his specific profession. Teachers, Doctors, Engineers, Politicians, Writers, Army, Police, Judges, Lawyers, Industrialists, Laborers, Skilled Workers, Farmers, Traders and Government Workers are included in this.

7. Defense, and Jihad with Sword

Jihad primarily means battle of thoughts and ideas which needs to be triumphed. Thoughts are communicated through words and words put together formulate a language, so consequently language is the vehicle of thought and thoughts are the source of power.

A very important aspect of Jihad is its spiritual aspect such as the purity of intent and outwardly cleanliness and enjoining the good deeds and forbidding the evil. We will gradually prepare for any confrontation and fight with sword against the disbelievers and that includes fighting by our assets and by our ownselves.

Warfare is one of the fundamental aspects of human life. Islam distinguishes itself uniquely in this stratum because it does not permit any aggression. The sole purpose of war preparation in Islam is defense and the ultimate goal of a believer is martyrdom. Fighting is only resorted to if Muslim Ummah is confronted and there is a danger to the life, property or sovereignty of Muslim states. Proper arrangements for war material, new techniques and trainings will be made. All public will participate in this. This will be done under the management of Government and the Army.

Our Army will have to adopt Islamic code of conduct according to the constitution of Pakistan. They will have to properly and fully act upon Islamic injunctions and teachings. Otherwise it will be a violation of the constitution of Pakistan. The entire nation will have to prepare for Jihad according to Islamic injunctions.

This is not the job of Army alone, but it is the call of the day that the whole nation should prepare for it. We will have to adapt such ethical and spiritual ways and acts of wisdom that can overcome our material and scientific weaknesses. The whole nation will work collectively and with singleness of purpose and there will be no space for cowardice, laziness, hypocrisy, deceit, conspiracy and treachery in this. Weapons of mass destruction will not be allowed to be made or to be used. Moreover civil defense bodies will be developed and promoted.

8. Organizational Structure, Politics and Constitutional Objectives

All Praise be to Allah! This is a clear and compulsory requirement of the constitution of the God given country of Pakistan that all affairs be managed according to Islamic injunctions and teachings. We will select only honest, capable and efficient persons for political affairs and national organization. They will manage and supervise affairs in their respective areas and fields and undertake training and organization of people with mutual consultation. All matters will be managed/ decided under a leader/ Ameer (who should be pious, wise, efficient, honest and capable) through a mutual consultation process in conformity to modern and traditional requirements.

This work will be undertaken on a Neighborhood, Tehsil, District, National, Regional and International level. Freedom will be given for all permitted, individual and collective deeds which are according to Islam, Quran and Sunnah and which do not harm Ummah's interest and resources.

We will strictly observe the rule that in future all acts will be performed in accordance to the Islamic way and within the limits set by Islam.

We reject the political parties system given by the British, which is a cause of discord, loot and injustice and will instead form a National Government based on natural rules of the society. It will be free from un-Islamic ways like desire to rule, lies, false accusations and material desires and based on Islamic ways. All that gives rise to discord and strife and becomes a cause of injustice and a source of tyranny, whether it is political, sectarian, nationalistic, class based or ideological, whatever is against the Muslim Ummah or gives rise to strife, will be eliminated. All secret or open plans to distort the right form of religion will be failed.

In the end it should be clarified that women have a special responsibility in all these affairs and they will have to play an important role in these matters (in accordance to Quran and Sunnah). Children, Old and victims will be fully protected according to Islam. Non-Muslims belonging to every section of society will fully participate in their respective fields as per their capabilities.

IS THERE A WAY OUT? (A Discourse on Democracy)

My Dear Brothers and Sisters,

Once again our nation is at a critical point in time where historical decisions shaping fate of a nation are taken. Whether it is the internal feuds or the external threats, the situation of our country is precarious. Most of our fellow men are distressed and weighed down with anxiety. (For all we know they just might be paying price for their deeds and thoughts, after all what goes around comes around), and are in search of a Messianic Light that might guide them out of the engulfing darkness and despair, and give them a ray of hope and happiness, making its way into their hearts so that the withered buds of hearts bloom once again basking in the light of faith, hope and happiness, and life becomes a good affair, and living it a cheerful prospect.

You should not only understand and acknowledge, but also make a strong determination of the fact that it is you, only you who have to take the first step towards your progress and improvement. These changes can be brought about only through the purity of our intentions, the love pulsating in our hearts, knowledge and good deeds, wisdom and understanding, through augmentation of our thoughts, by discipline and organization, and last but not the least, by having the spirit of sacrifice and practice of patience and tolerance. However falling prey to hopelessness and mental perplexity will definitely be a hindrance in the way of achieving these goals. Man gets only what he strives for, and Allah Almighty has never brought a change in a nation's condition, unless they themselves aim for it and strive for it. Allah has bestowed on humans the power to take the right decisions, on the basis of reason and sincerity, besides continuous determination and diligence with faith and belief (in Allah and in ourselves). The nations that keep their hopes high and their priorities right are showered with blessings and success by the Almighty, while alternatively calamities and tragedies become their destiny.

With purity of intention and sincerity of feelings, I am bringing up all this because once again the fate of you country and people lies to some extent in your hands! If the circumstances remained favorable and elections are held on time, then you yourselves will be deciding your fates. All the difficulties and troubles befalling you as the result of wrong decisions taken will be only your responsibility.

80% of the total population of this country comprises of people who are in no way involved in politics, neither do they belong to any political party nor are they political workers. Political parties all they do is that they present their candidates and their manifesto before the masses and employ all fair and unfair means and resources to achieve their agendas. But the important point is that we should look beyond what a political party says or claims and perceive the broader picture debating different problems, matters and principles. Eventually it is our country, and democratic principles require that masses take part in the affairs of country with obligation and integrity.

The question arises here, what is our objective and what sort of government do we want?

1) We aspire for a system whose basic ideology rests on the fact that absolute sovereignty belongs to the one and the only One Allah. This is an integral part of our constitution too. Our Creator in whose hands are the reigns of everything and in whose complete control is the functioning and destiny of everything. He is the Omnipotent, the One to whom we turn to for our final and absolute decisions. The one who is the Creator and the Sustainer, the all Knowing, the all Wise. Man has been created only to obey and worship Him. He is the One who determines right and wrong, the permissible the forbidden in all levels of individual and collective life. He is the ultimate source of peace and harmony.

2) The second basic rule should be that Allah's last Prophet (p.b.u.h) is the best example for us and his teachings are a complete code to succeed in life. "The Sunnah" (sayings and deeds of the Prophet) teaches us wisdom, knowledge, purity, independent reasoning, truth, sincerity in our actions and deeds.

3) Allah sent human beings as His representative and emissary; all the forces of nature have been deferred for him. He granted us knowledge and the ability to think rationally, and clearly marked the difference between right and wrong, good and evil. He granted man with all the blessings to test how he will fulfill his duties with purity of faith, love, and fear of Allah, loyalty, discipline, wisdom, patience, courage and resilience. And consequently either attains the loftiest of ranks in life or collapses into the deepest trenches of regression.

4) Holy Quran, an exemplary, highly authentic and respectable book was revealed to us for our guidance, telling us the difference between right and wrong. Understanding and following the Holy Quran is a duty implemented on us. It is a promise, an oath which we have to fulfill. This temporary world will eventually come to an end, after which we will face our Creator and give account for all our actions. There justice shall prevail! Bad deeds shall be punished and good deeds shall be rewarded. That is the reason that both on individual and collective level, it is the duty of the government to be virtuous and follow the rules set by Allah and keeps the national harmony intact.

5) All major decisions should be taken through consensus of opinion and opinions should be sought only from those people who are pious and abstain from sins, and those who establish prayers and give zakat (charity).

6) Conflict and chaos should be put to an end.

7) Good should be enjoined and wrong be forbidden.

8) People should help each other in noble and virtuous deeds.

9) The commands of the government should be followed honestly, sincerely and efficiently.

10) All matters should be dealt with justice and sincerity of intentions.

11) Life, honor and wealth of the citizens should be protected. Law should be upheld and order and restraint be maintained. The criminals should be punished aptly and in time.

12) Equality and brotherhood should be promoted.

13) Basic needs should be fulfilled. Orphans, widows, helpless and the needy should be helped and taken care of.

14) Rulers of the nation should be the servers (servants).

15) Everybody should be equal in the eyes of law. Rulers should be accountable to the law too.

16) Rulers should be trustworthy, sincere, honest, wise, strong, brave, kind, dignified, patriotic, generous and humble.

17) Rulers should be approachable to the masses.

18) People should not run after official positions.

19) Moderation and good sense should be assumed.

20) People should aspire to become role models for others.

21) Freedom of religion. Freedom of expression should be allowed for the spread of benevolence. Tolerance and mutual understanding should be fostered.

22) Promises and commitments should be fulfilled.

23) Peace and harmony should prevail. Fighting and killings should not be approved unless necessary i.e. to curb the evil and inhibit the conflict in a systematic and legitimate manner.

24) Punishments might be given but according to the nature of the crime and the judiciary should be independent and free of all pressure. Rehabilitation and forgiveness are to be urged.

25) State has to be free of prejudice towards different groups, ethnicities and classes. Affairs should be dealt on the basis of God fearing and merit and capability. Law must not allow attainment of personal benefits, bribery, and using contacts to get one's way, corruption, dishonesty, theft, violence, vulgarity, alcoholism, drugs, interest, adultery, perjury and bearing of false witness. Laws should be formulated for the elimination of all these vices, whose implementation will be the responsibility of the government so that mutual love, trust and truthfulness flourish.

26) Spread of knowledge, industrialization and progress in the fields of science should take place.

27) Government is to be responsible for the material, spiritual and educational development of its people.

28) Taxes should be enacted justly. Public treasury should not be used wastefully, and be fairly spent on crucial and important projects.

29) Defense of the country should be strong and impassable.

Dear friends! To have such a government must be your heartfelt desire, if not everybody's but definitely must be the majority's wish and aspiration. It is hard to nurture an optimistic thought like this through these dark times. It seems like a far-fetched dream which would perhaps never be realized but losing hope is parallel to losing faith. Although man is a sinner but he is inclined towards accepting goodness, when presented to him. Even though humans make mistakes every day, they can always ask for Allah's forgiveness. The Merciful One's benevolence is calling out to His slaves to revert back to Him, where never-ending happiness and prosperity of the both worlds are awaiting them.

The question that arises is how did we reach our current state? How did we come by such state? What is the reality of present day situation?

The sum-up of reasons of political turmoil in the Muslim world are as follows: Firstly we haven't been able to devise an appropriate way of transfer of power till now, and this has led to loss of our precious strength and many valuable and capable individuals. Secondly there has always been a clash between the rulers and the clergy, and they have moved away from each other and in some instances became involved in internal conspiracies against each other. Thirdly masses have been lacking political awareness and missing cultivation of democratic conduct. The nation has not been able to tell between the sincere and the duplicitous, and the incapable were assumed as leaders. They have been bearing all the injustices inflicted upon them, and have ignored all their misconduct thus obstructing the way of those who are sincere, capable and honest. Other than this, the nation has failed to act rationally and rise above the prejudices of state, nation and race. Administrative matters became muddled. Politics and knowledge came to a stand-still. People were no longer enthusiastic about the prospect of finding new ways; rather they were transfixed on sectarian and selfish interests. They have been lured by the western scams. And then fate bestowed upon us, leaders who either did not have the best interest of country at heart or who had an altogether different set of principles, which they tried to impose upon people. Consequently the people forgot the little they knew about themselves and became all confused and disheveled. If we look around ourselves, the nations that have made progress even though merely material advancement, are the ones who haven't let go of their individuality. While those following blindly and mindlessly were repressed just like us.

The answer to all these problems is said to be democracy. Let us analyze our present situation with this view point too.

One important aspect of the political history of present world is that democracy has been generally accepted as a better and popular system. Even the developing countries have adopted democracy as the system of government. Recently, the communist block has affirmed democracy as the guiding principle in their policy making. In our country too, except for the times of martial law, we are ruled by a parliamentary form of government.

The basic principle of democracy is that the majority of public participates and is given due representation in the administration of matters of society and the state. And that the reforms be made with the unanimous approval and consent of all classes and the public. Democracy also recognizes the differences, and favors the formation of different classes, programs, groups, and factions. Democracy helps to put a boundary between accountability and the interests of different strata of society. In theory, it is an easy and most appropriate form of government but knowing from experience we know that there are many practical obstacles and hurdles and dangers in it. It is no easy job to formulate an effective, just and feasible democratic system.

With respect to Pakistan, democracy is even harder to implement because of the formation of many power hubs due to the historical process. Regional, factional, religious, societal, geographical, and historical factors determine either the progression or the regression of our political life's destiny. Any individual with an insight cannot ignore the fact that these factors affect our society both directly and indirectly. Also the illiteracy and backwardness of our majority cannot be overlooked.

Unfortunately we have taken democracy as an unalterable holy text that cannot change with time and circumstances. We have closed all the doors of its evolution. We think that in order to achieve the higher objectives of democracy, we have to preserve it as it is at all costs. In-fact democracy has been gradually evolving, since the times of Greece's democratic states to the parliamentarian system of West; it has passed through many developmental stages. Philosophers, thinkers, reformers and politicians, in fact people from all walks of life have been improving this system. No system with all its constituents can be affirmed as definitive as it would cause it to stagnate. Human mind is progressing through constant change which is persistent and unyielding. Any system bearing the merits of progress and efficiency, will be analyzing different sorts and come across new experiences. Surely it will be based on fundamental principles and life experiences.

If we carefully examine the present democratic system, we come across different questions and slip-ups which are summarized as follows:

The first question we ask is that what will determine the scale of majority and its representation. A person may win in any constituency with a slight majority and sometimes even the total amount of nominally cast votes might declare him as the winner because the votes are divided. Consequently a large number of voters are denied the right of representation.

Very few segments of the society can succeed in the present electoral system, whereas a large number of people cannot be a part of this system due to different problems and complications.

In this era of science and technology where we employ various scientific methods to make important decisions, we rely on the majority for critical decision making; even though the majority might not be able to comprehend the delicacy of matters. Instead of being thoroughly deliberated and reflected upon decisions that determine the fates of nations are inspired by slogans and emotions.

We have also seen that almost half of the registered voters do not cast their votes at all, thus the represented opinion is actually representative of only a minority. Due to lack of education and knowledge, the casting voters do not know the essentials and importance of matters. There is no system to make the candidates acquainted and determine their eligibility, experience and education etc. In fact there is no method to define or analyze any capabilities whatsoever. In national and provincial assemblies where the representative constituencies are quite large this problem becomes more complex.

It has been also observed that very often people only vote for a candidate belonging to their own specific area, group or province which creates various problems for the federation endangering the whole system to collapse. What we are in need of is that plans should be formulated to reform politics and system of the government so as to ensure that discrepancies can be ruled out and problems be sorted out. However, in our present democratic system, all our time and energies are devoted to the unnecessary frivolities of long pompous and ponderous speeches, public appearances and swanky images. And after the elections, attempts to keep the supporters happy, and humiliating the opponents are the top priority proceedings. Thus our leaders are left with very less time to build or work for the nation and the country.

The independent candidates become saleable commodities. Nobody abides by the pledges of loyalty to their respective parties. They are ready to grease anybody's palm, even for the slightest hope of getting a position or monetary benefits. Whoever offers more money can have their souls. In our dear country, anybody found guilty of such despicable acts should be dealt with like ordinary thieves. They should be presented in the courts of civil magistrate and should be remanded to police custody. Confessions should be extorted out of them by all means. The embezzled money should be confiscated and deposited in the treasury. They should be sentenced to rigorous imprisonment for peddling public's trust. Otherwise democracy will come to a standstill.

Let us now review some suggestions for the evolution and improvement of this system, and we might as well be successful in making it better still.

Parties should be restricted to nominate only a certain number of candidates from any region or province. In this way the parties who have a regional base will be discouraged. In the same way the ruling party should also be able to get at least a certain number of votes, from every region or province.

The distribution of resources, whether between the provinces or districts or different classes of the country, should be done justly through a fair system. These principles should be formulated after reviewing them for their practicality and scientific application. They should not be compromised on the altar of personal or factional ego of a person or a group.

Ministers should be allowed positions according to their experience and eligibility. Also they should be citizens with spotless character and their broad experience should guarantee success.

Professional courses should be devised to instill in them legislative procedures and conventions. Parties should train their people to become capable of delivering their optimal performance and not giving the bureaucrats an eye for the chance, after taking up these ranks.

The whole nation should be given education. It should extend over a period of at least twelve years, so as to elude partial illiteracy. During this time they should be made capable of becoming completely aware of their rights and duties.

The elected government should be above partiality i.e. benefiting constituencies that voted in the government's favor with development projects, and disregarding and paying no attention to the anti-government areas. There should be development plans on a plane for the whole country. Similarly public treasury should not be treated as the entitlement of ministers and party members who toss it away as their birth right. There should be no unfairness in allocations of jobs as well as business contracts and tenders. Similarly in all fields, the deserving should get what they deserve.

Politicians should sit down with politics and management specialists to devise a system for bringing forth suggestions about the modification and evolvement of the present system of democracy in order to create such harmony and peace in the country which will ensure equal opportunities for all. And politics will once again become a tool of service to the people instead of a trade.

It has been commonly observed that democratic process is brought to a halt for without any sound reason just because some hoodwinks, along with their cronies will insist on generating chaos, anarchy, hooliganism, murdering, plundering, plotting, scheming, aiding foreign interference and other such nasty tactics so that the common man is forced to become a mere spectator, whereas these hooligans achieve what they set out for; an unobstructed path between a common man and their vested interests. This give rise to duplicity and there seems to be no way out of it. A common man would want to bare their faces and expose these people who are pushing the country into an abyss of despair and disappointment, but sincere and capable people are forced to stand by and watch in helplessness.

Eventually it happens so is that when the politicians are unable to fulfill their duties and when the masses are fed up with their actions, then establishment and the military takes control of the country, using political unrest as their excuse (which is genuine to an extent) and the others testing their lucks. It is obvious that this can only be a temporary solution and everybody is aware of its long term disadvantages, as it doubles up the duties of military and establishment, which can affect their performance too. After all, how can a non-elected body rule the country on long-term basis and that too successfully? Eventually we will have to device a system in this country. For how long will the people be hurled between the politicians and the army in order to get their requirements fulfilled which gives rise to injustices, disparities, bigotry, transgressions and violence, and we have been through this situation several times.

At this point yours, mine's and everybody's duty commences. To think, that what can we possibly do is essentially WRONG. If you can get rid of governments and dissolve assemblies, take out rallies and cause conflict and strive for every wrong and right, then how can you be not held accountable for national development. Remember that we are reaping fruits of this kind of thinking. We cannot sit back and wait for some other beings to help us in our plight, because that is Not going to happen. You and I are going to take the country ahead towards progress and betterment with our little efforts.

Friends! You are well aware of the fact that many a little makes a mickle. You all must have definitely observed that courage, perseverance and collective effort can fetch surprising results and still when you are given a chance to vote then why do we make the wrong decisions most of the time? There are many reasons for this, which are mostly related to our way of thinking and our national psyche.

First of all, it has been statistically proven that about 50 to 60% of total aggregate do not even cast their vote! Keep in mind that this does not include the unregistered voters. Why this thoughtlessness? When the country's fate is at stake, when the course of our lives is about to change, when our future generations are to be affected and when it is the matter of our pride and dignity among the nations of the world and we do not even bother to cast our votes, and that too without any lucid reason. I believe this is a big mistake, and you are neglecting a very major duty. You might say that the candidates are not competent and we are not satisfied with them. You are right that men of character have become a novelty and it has become hard to find good people. But we will have to find a solution, because if we don't, then these incapable people will soon be holding the reins of our country. It is not fitting that you leave the field, open and undefended, so that these greedy, shrewd and immoral people can get a chance to come onward and rule.

We will have to get over this weakness. We will have to demonstrate moral courage and the spirit of sacrificing otherwise the right to command shall remain with the unworthy. But if the state of affairs is such that all the candidates are formidable, compelling and not credible enough then in accordance with the Holy Prophet's (p.b.u.h) Hadith, we acquire the lesser evil. If however it is due to thoughtlessness then for God's sake change this attitude, and if it is due to fear and vulnerability then try to somehow overcome this state of fearfulness and helplessness. After all, all human beings are dependent on each other, in one way or another. No person can be all authoritative and commanding. This kind of might and supremacy is for Allah alone.

This message is for those who do not cast their votes at all. You form such a huge majority therefore you should step in and you can play a role in bringing forward much better people, and surely by Allah's will state of affairs will change. In this context another important thing to be mentioned is that casting vote is not the sole problem. Casting vote to the right and committed person is what matters. This is your responsibility to bring forward in your meetings better people from different parties or people who in your opinion are worthier, even though they do not belong to any party. They should be of the right attitude and best bearing and they should be capable and should have all the traits of a leader. (As wrong-doing actually starts when political parties give tickets to incompetent people). You should hold competitions between better people. Apparently this is difficult to say that all the upright and virtuous people belong to the same party or organization and all the decadent and corrupt people to the other. But if you will, you can systematically bring forward the righteous and noble people from all the parties and promulgate basis for clean politics and healthy competition. There can be differences in view-points and their relevance but this does not mean that all will go awry. If we have a look at the developed nations where democratic process has sufficiently matured up, every party holds open conventions for the nominations of representatives before the elections and they give a lot of importance to these nominations.

Let's talk about people whose uncalled-for kindness result in the imposition of incapable people on us, who are a disaster for the country, its resources and its destiny, resulting in final destruction of all of us. Every human being has, at least, the basic sense of what is good and what is bad. Still we must evaluate the criteria of assessment of candidates. One thing I would like to state here is that our people have a very queer temperament. They are either in search of an angel, who is devoid of any flaw. However it is quite clear that, this perfection can only be attributed to Allah. Finding the most perfect person on human level is difficult indeed in a vast society. And this is a fact too that even the word "insaan" (human) means imperfect and guilty at fault. Even the best amongst us can err, but this is where we shut our minds and are not ready to accept reality. We must take into account character of a man as a whole; if he steers clear of major sins, if he is trustworthy, capable, wise and fair, then we will have to ignore the minor wrong-doings. But when we fail to find our ideal idol, then we lose track of things in utter disappointment and we bow down to any vagabond and thug who comes forward to take charge of us and we follow them blindly. We reap as we sow. Actually the bit of evil we all have inside us also plays a part here. When we feel the urge to follow the wrong, we blame everything on the extinction of good people (which is not true!)

If there are no more good people, this world would have destroyed. And when we suffer at the hands of the selected representatives, we start complaining and criticizing. But it is quite clear that how can you hope for any good from dishonest and characterless people

Besides all this, three things affect the thinking and decision of the voters. The first and the most essential thing which we come across in our daily lives and most importantly during the days of the elections is group partiality, on the basis of which votes are casted. Many have written in favor of and many against this biased approach. A lot has already been written. Here I will only say that do fight for your rights but do not be prejudiced. Do not stoop to levels of injustice, violence and ignorance. Keep it in check. After all other men are your brothers. They too are humans like you. They too are comprised of good and bad just like you. Criteria should be based on merit not on prejudice. Factions, color, race, language, nationality and classes, they all constitute such fixations that we even forget injunctions of our Lord and our beloved Prophet (peace be upon him) and basic human values.

Remember, even two groups can arrive on a decision in harmony and tackle affairs brilliantly, which will result in tangible and long-lasting mutual benefit. This can be achieved when members of both groups are men of character, principled and capable, who tackle their problems in a just and straightforward manner, even if the decision goes against their benefits. In such matters wrong thinking result in discord, disharmony and weakness which might result in sinking of the whole ship. What a logic it is that one of the onboard, drills a hole on the other side of the ship thinking that those on the other side will perish, but he will survive! Isn't it obvious that when a ship sinks it takes down everything with it into the water; it doesn't differentiate between this side and that side. To fight for our rights is the correct thing to do, but not at the cost of rebelling against Allah Almighty and His Prophet (P.B.U.H) and being unkind and pitiless towards others.

Thirdly, keeping in mind our personal and timely gains also tend to affect whom do we choose to vote. Sometimes these gains are in the form of paper money. What should I say about that? It is pretty obvious that this action depicts a weak character, lack of intellect and greed and it gives a golden opportunity to swindlers and raiders of public resources. These people buy your precious votes for a meager amount, and after being positioned they consider it their birth right to loot the country's treasury and top up their accounts relishing in their glory, while leaving us miserable in our own plight.

The purpose of delivering this message to you is that the next time you cast your vote; you shall know the sacredness of it and the role it will be playing in deciding the future of our country. Please understand these guidelines, use them and spread this message to all those who are less fortunate and unaware.

CHAPTER 6

UOB Division Four

ASSOCIA- Methods for Improving Mutually Beneficial Organizational and Individual Lives.

As the CORE and all its organizations will be working at a second level, ASSOCIA redundantly will act.

It will be the mirror image of CORE because we will have to take along with ourselves the existing organizations and people, because creating out of nothing is something which only Allah can do, not any human being. Because of this chances of error will be almost zero.

It is an established scientific principle that if you get one information which is from a single source which is 70 % correct, chances of errors are 51%, whereas the same information with the same level of accuracy if obtained from a second source the chances of error are 1 in billion. (Hadith)

So ASSOCIA breaks the pyramidal model and goes into biological model.

2nd principle again proved mathematically (which is the highest form of human intellect possible) that greater the diversity of a system and greater the variety it can handle, more are the chances of improvement in that system. So through ASSOCIA we are bringing the diversity and variety in our model of UOB to an ultimate level (See works of Norvid Weiner and Stafford Bear in this regard). This is method through which the system keeps itself in control which keeps it alive growing and evolving and avoids rigidity which is bound to crack. Readers who are more interested can find it in the works of control systems, decision making and real modeling of system behavior. So we are going to put forward a list of as many aspects of human life as possible and bring them closer into an intra and interdisciplinary relationship.

Another basic principle of nature is duality in everything. If there is darkness there is light, everything in the universe exist as pairs, the binary system, yes-no, yes-no which are the fundamental building blocks of Human society. I will not bother the reader with more of this but I am only trying to give him an easy to understand model based in life time research as my capacity as an Electrical and Nuclear Engineer in these fields.

Note the first diagram which you have seen, we will follow it by a three dimensional diagram to make it multi layered and mirror images of each other. This will keep the balance and equilibrium so essential for the survival.